LANCASHIRE CRICKET LEGENDS

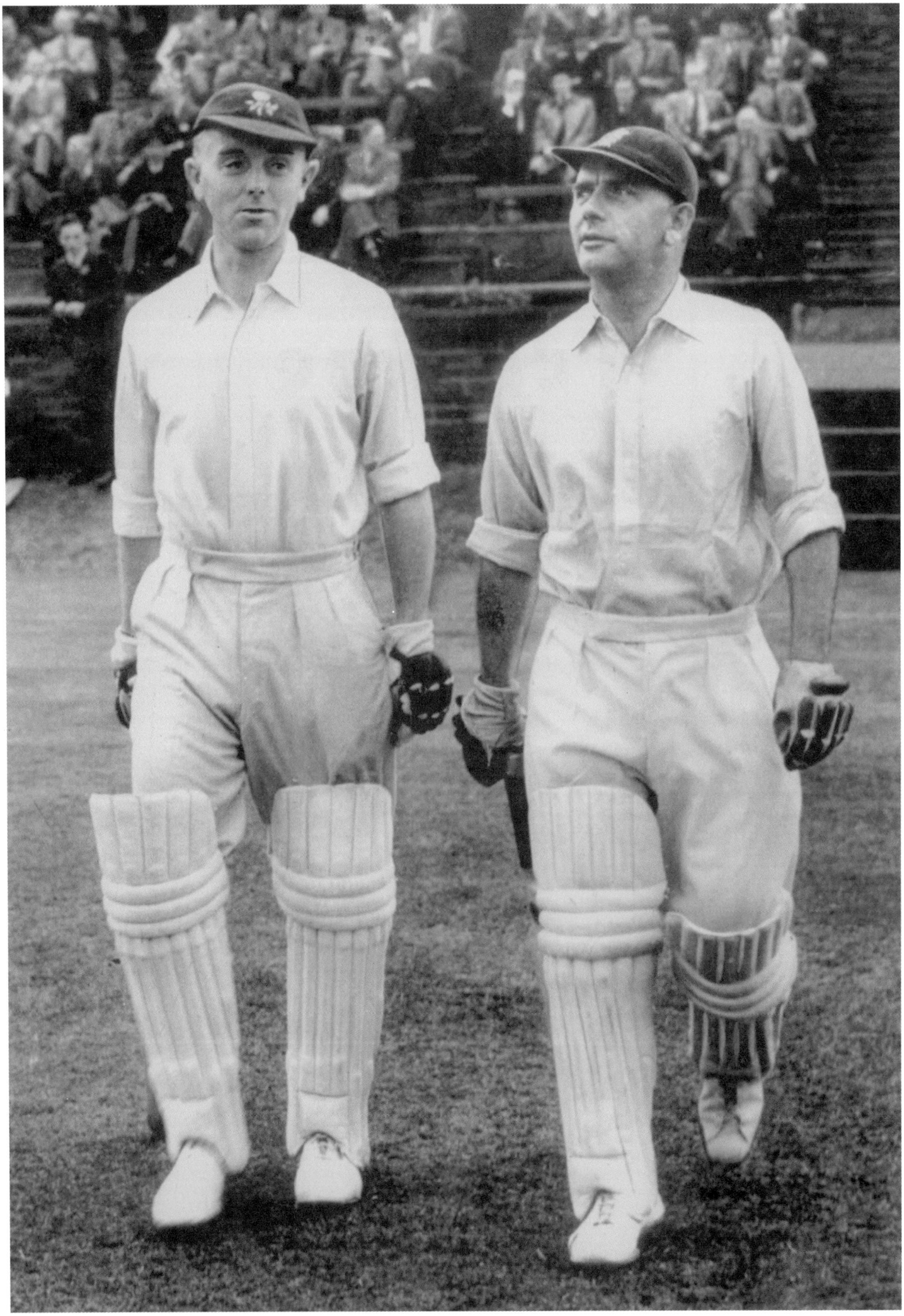

Lancashire Cricket Legends

Since 1946

Dean P. Hayes

Foreword by Jack Bond

Sutton Publishing

Sutton Publishing Limited
Phoenix Mill · Thrupp · Stroud
Gloucestershire · GL5 2BU

First published 2002

Copyright © Dean P. Hayes, 2002

Cover illustrations: Front: Michael Atherton, Ken Grieves, David Lloyd, Paul Allott, Mike Watkinson, Bob Berry. Back: Farokh Engineer, Mike Watkinson. (LEP)

Half-title page photograph: Benson & Hedges Cup final team, 1995. (LEP)

Frontispiece: Winston Place (left) and Cyril Washbrook. (MEN)

British Library Cataloguing in Publication Data
A catalogue record for this book is available from the British Library.

ISBN 0-7509-2969-3

Typeset in 10.5/13.5 Photina.
Typesetting and origination by
Sutton Publishing Limited.
Printed and bound in England by
J.H. Haynes & Co. Ltd, Sparkford.

(All pictures LEP)

Contents

Foreword by Jack Bond 6
Introduction 7

The Legends

Paul Allott
Michael Atherton
Bob Barber
Bob Berry
Jack Bond
Ken Cranston
John Crawley
Geoff Edrich
Farokh Engineer
Neil Fairbrother
Graeme Fowler
Tommy Greenhough
Ken Grieves
Frank Hayes
Ken Higgs
Malcolm Hilton
Nigel Howard
David Hughes

Jack Ikin
Peter Lever
Clive Lloyd
David Lloyd
Peter Marner
Harry Pilling
Winston Place
Dick Pollard
Geoff Pullar
Ken Shuttleworth
Jack Simmons
Brian Statham
Roy Tattersall
Cyril Washbrook
Wasim Akram
Mike Watkinson
Alan Wharton
Barry Wood

And then there's . . .

John Abrahams
Ian Austin
Glen Chapple

Warren Hegg
Peter Lee
Peter Martin

Best XI 123
Statistics 124
Acknowledgements & Picture Credits 128

Foreword

by Jack Bond

When crowds flocked back to watch cricket after the war, many of the players performed so consistently in front of thousands that they became the subject of conversation over a drink and became household names. Old Trafford was being rebuilt after the Royal Engineers had requisitioned the ground during the war. Most of the players were in uniform but in reasonable shape to start making individual contributions to the game, frustrated at the massive loss of six seasons.

The magnificent summer of 1947 set new records in the sun and Lancashire players, like those at other counties, reaped the benefit of continuous play, good batting surfaces and bumper crowds to support and give atmosphere. Washbrook and Place became established opening partners as they rolled out a thousand runs a season. Their popularity was expressed by the record benefit given to Washbrook – in relative terms, as big a gift as any benefit total to date. He set a tone for the new era, that famous confident strut with cap at jaunty angle to announce that Lancashire were open for business.

After sharing the Championship in 1950 it took the one day game to inspire a team of all rounders to achieve deserved honours. Trophies came in abundance from the late '60s, there was a hat-trick of Gillette cup wins in the '70s and in the '90s Lancashire became the first county to achieve the double of one-day major trophies. Talented all rounders abounded from the early days: Jack Simmons and David Hughes, David Lloyd, Barry Wood and Mike Watkinson. They were excellent fielders too and were joined by overseas players who had great presence on the field – Farokh Engineer, Clive Lloyd and Wasim Akram. Alongside talented Lancashire players like Neil Fairbrother, Michael Atherton, Graeme Fowler and John Crawley, they created a winning formula.

Cricket is a team game but also a game of individuals and this book reflects on many of the talented cricketers who represented Lancashire and brought it success after the war. I was coached by the earliest, played with the majority of them and have prepared nets for the youngest. I am proud to be part of this great team of players who have graced Old Trafford.

Jack Bond

Introduction

The Second World War made severe inroads into the careers of Cyril Washbrook and Winston Place, who were on the verge of international cricket by 1939. The war also imperilled Old Trafford itself. Bomb craters scarred the turf, and pavilion, stands and the groundsman's house were severely damaged. Lives were lost.

When peace returned so did cricket. Old Trafford was repaired, Washbrook played for England and captained Lancashire. The ground renovation fund received a world-wide response and applications for county membership overflowed on to a waiting list. Reconstruction of the ground proved easier than reconstruction of a powerful team, however. Washbrook fulfilled all expectations with a 1946 average of 71.77 and he, Ikin and Pollard were chosen to tour Australia. They were joined at international level by Ken Cranston, a gifted player, who captained Lancashire for two seasons, but at this time the side as a whole lacked the resources for championship success.

Nigel Howard became captain in 1949 and the following year led Lancashire to become joint champions with Surrey. They started the 1950 season heavily dependent on the slow bowling of Roy Tattersall, Bob Berry and Malcolm Hilton but with their lack of a pace bowler, the county came under fire from allegations that they prepared wickets to suit their assets. Howard, Washbrook, Grieves, Place, Edrich, Wharton and Ikin all made runs while Tattersall, with 171 wickets at 13.29 runs each, and Hilton, with 127, were joined by a certain Brian Statham and made an impressive bowling line-up.

Lancashire finished third in seasons 1951 and 1952, featuring in a tied match at Brentwood against Essex in 1952. In 1953 Bob Berry took all 10 Worcestershire wickets at Blackpool, the first time since 1900 that a Lancashire player had achieved the feat.

Through the 1950s Lancashire's Championship record ranged from the praiseworthy to the disastrous, with correspondingly wide variations in public support. The administrators were called on at various times to defend their policies. Importation of players had always been challenged as a principle but the practice continued through the periods of debate. Lancashire consistently offered high reward, both financial and fraternal, for loyalty by adoptees and faithful service by natives. Wages were good and benefits exceptional by the standards of the time.

Dick Pollard and Jack Ikin were typical in the measure of service rendered and appreciation accorded. Pollard's advance as a fast-medium right-arm bowler was delayed by the war, but he took 1,015 wickets for Lancashire and played for England at home and overseas. Ikin was a left-handed batsman of resolute approach, a right-arm bowler of leg-breaks and googly, and a short-leg fieldsman of exceptional skill and daring.

Pollard and Ikin were succeeded in Lancashire and England favour by Brian Statham, whose fast bowling startled Yorkshire in their first meeting with him in 1950. Statham's talent was not advertised in his appearance. His nickname, 'Whippet', specified slim build and smooth approach, and no fast bowler could have seemed less menacing to the unwary. The illusion was completed with modest droop of the shoulders behind a belated bat. Most of his successes had to be twice-earned, for he was notoriously unlucky in missing the stumps or the edge of the bat and the consistency of his length and direction probably added to his own labour. Statham was a fast bowler of uncommonly equable temperament and inevitably he was called upon for more than his share of bowling. He dominated Lancashire's bowling until his retirement in 1968, by which time he had taken a record 1,816 wickets for Lancashire.

When Statham, Higgs and Greenhough all took 100 wickets in the summer of 1960 – the second successive year that all three achieved the feat – Lancashire finished second in the Championship. The county also unearthed two England opening batsmen in Bob Barber and Geoff Pullar, along with hard-hitting Peter Marner, who was the first winner of the man-of-the-match gold medal in the newly formed Gillette Cup. Pullar had the distinction of scoring the first Test hundred by a Lancastrian at Old Trafford when he hit 131 against India in 1959. But from being runners-up in 1960, Lancashire slipped to the bottom half of the table, stumbling their way through the 1960s; a special meeting of members in 1964 overthrew the committee. Statham captained the side in the closing years of his career and Higgs took 71 wickets in 15 Tests for England but not even the alliance of these two bowlers could make the county a force again in the game.

It was not until Jack Bond took over the captaincy in 1968 that Lancashire started to improve. They immediately moved up to sixth position in the County Championship but it was the introduction of the John Player League on Sundays, the instant cricket of 40 overs a side, that saw their full re-emergence as a force.

Lancashire had taken full advantage of the new registration rules governing overseas players to sign Farokh Engineer, the Indian wicket-keeper, and West Indian Clive Lloyd. Bond built a new young side, brilliant in the field. They were such fine exponents of the limited-overs game that they won the John Player League in its first two seasons, 1969 and 1970. And they just missed a hat-trick of wins by losing the last two matches of the 1971 Sunday League. Lancashire also dominated the Gillette Cup in the 1970s, winning through to the final at Lord's six times in seven years and coming away with the trophy in 1970, 1971, 1972 and 1975.

In 1970, one of Lancashire's finest-ever seasons, the county were in with the possibility of winning all three trophies on offer. Sadly, the one trophy which eluded them was the Championship: their final position was third. Bad weather over the last couple of fixtures was a decisive factor. The summer of 1971 was similar. Lancashire finished third in the Championship again and for the first time did not win the Sunday League, although if they had beaten Glamorgan on the last afternoon of the competition, they would have. They retained the Gillette Cup with a six-wicket win over Sussex. The crowds flocked back to Old Trafford, capacity gates were attracted to all Sunday League and Gillette Cup matches, the most memorable of which was the semi-final against Gloucestershire when David Hughes hit 24 runs off a John Mortimore over in a game that went on until 8.50 p.m.

After Lancashire won the Gillette Cup for a third time in 1972, Jack Bond retired, leaving the county overflowing with success and support. Frank Hayes, David Lloyd, Peter Lever, Ken Shuttleworth and Barry Wood all played for England and Harry Pilling was unlucky not to

Barry Wood

Farokh Engineer

Paul Allott

Peter Martin

(All pictures LEP)

do so. With Cedric Rhoades as chairman, Old Trafford regained its prominent place in English cricket. But the team gradually broke up and the county slipped back to a permanent place in the bottom half of the Championship. There was another threat to the committee, but this time it was rebutted.

Jack Bond returned to the club as manager in 1980 and four years later Lancashire had their first success in nine seasons when, under John Abrahams' captaincy, they won the Benson & Hedges Cup. Two recruits from Durham University, the stylish left-handed opener Graeme Fowler and the accurate opening bowler Paul Allott, both capped in 1981, went on to play for England.

After captaining the side from 1981 to 1983, Clive Lloyd resumed for 1986 but only played in seven County Championship matches. Chairman Cedric Rhoades resigned and former player Bob Bennett replaced him. Rhoades had done a magnificent job for Lancashire County Cricket Club, the Old Trafford ground and its facilities being a lasting testimony to the former chairman who died in 1990.

David Hughes was appointed Lancashire captain for 1987. At the end of his first season he was voted Captain of the Year by the Cricket Writers' Club and became one of *Wisden*'s Five Cricketers of the Year. Though the county had a poor season in the three limited-overs competitions, they came within a whisker of winning the County Championship, falling four points short of the title. Paul Allott and Jack Simmons had a great season with the ball, while wicket-keeper Warren Hegg impressed behind the stumps.

The arrival of Pakistan Test all-rounder Wasim Akram was a boost to the side and after winning the Refuge Assurance Cup in 1988, Lancashire won the Refuge Assurance League the following year. Wasim Akram broke the Sunday wicket haul for Lancashire with 27, while Neil Fairbrother led the way with the runs.

The summer of 1990 will go down as the year when Lancashire made and broke almost all the records. In the County Championship Neil Fairbrother and Michael Atherton broke the county third wicket record with a stand of 364 against Surrey at The Oval: Fairbrother scored 366 while Atherton finished on 191. Lancashire's 863 was the county's highest-ever score while Surrey's 707 for 9 was the highest score against LCCC. Second place in the Sunday League was softened somewhat by Graeme Fowler breaking the county's Sunday record with 773 runs.

In the Benson & Hedges Cup, the match against Hampshire at Old Trafford was called off due to bad weather but Lancashire still broke all records with 352 for 6. Fairbrother and Atherton added 244 for the third wicket. Sadly, because of the inclement weather, the record did not stand. Lancashire went on to beat Worcestershire in the final by 69 runs with Mike Watkinson deservedly winning the man-of-the-match award. Lancashire also won the NatWest Trophy (the successor to the Gillette Cup), beating Northamptonshire by seven wickets. A destructive spell of fast bowling by Phil de Freitas reduced Lancashire's opponents to 39 for 5.

In 1991, having taken all the one-day trophies under Hughes, Lancashire went all-out to win the County Championship, but sadly the wheels came off and the side finished in eighth place. Neil Fairbrother replaced Hughes as captain but in 1992 and 1993 his form suffered as the county endured two mediocre seasons. All-rounder Mike Watkinson replaced the popular left-hander as captain for 1994, a season which saw John Crawley top the county's batting averages with 1,300 runs at 61.90. He was also voted Young Cricketer of the Year.

Mike Watkinson (right) and a young Andrew Flintoff, now England's most promising all-rounder and Lancashire's vice captain for 2002. (LEP)

In 1995 Watkinson led Lancashire to victory in the Benson & Hedges Cup as they beat Kent by 35 runs and to fourth place in the County Championship. In 1996 Lancashire retained the Benson & Hedges Cup by beating Northamptonshire by 31 runs; Ian Austin, an unsung hero for the county down the years, won the man-of-the-match award with 4 for 21 and he and Neil Fairbrother (with 63) were the stars of a fairly low-key final. The county also won the NatWest Trophy in one of the freakiest of all Lord's finals. John Crawley's innings of 66, some 45 runs more than any other batsman achieved, was an exceptionally skilful effort as Lancashire totalled 186. Peter Martin and Glen Chapple used the conditions superbly and Essex were skittled out for just 57. Chapple's return of 6 for 18 is the best ever in a Lord's county final.

After mediocre seasons in 1997 and 1998 Wasim Akram was appointed captain and, in what proved to be his sole season in charge, Lancashire won the NatWest Trophy and the Sunday League as well as finishing runners-up to Leicestershire in the County Championship. Although it took the red rose county until 1 p.m. on the second day to extend their record tally of Gillette Cup and NatWest Trophy titles to seven, Lancashire's demolition of Derbyshire was achieved in a mere 67 overs, the shortest of all the September showpieces. Derbyshire were bowled out for 108 with Martin (4 for 19) and Austin (3 for 14) sharing the spoils. Though Dominic Cork removed Atherton's off-stump, Fairbrother and Crawley saw Lancashire home with almost half their overs in hand – it was fitting that Neil Fairbrother, appearing in a Lord's final for a record tenth time, should make the winning hit.

Sri Lankan spin wizard Muttiah Muralitharan joined the county halfway through the summer of 1999 and in just seven matches he took 66 wickets at 11.77 runs apiece, including match figures of 14 for 117 on his debut against Warwickshire at Southport. Lancashire were again runners-up in the County Championship but with John Crawley now at the helm, they won the first-ever CGU National League title. During the course of the competition, they amassed 301 for 6 against Essex at Chelmsford with Andy Flintoff completing his 100 off just 50 balls.

Lancashire were runners-up in the County Championship for the third successive season in 2000, finishing 20 points behind champions Surrey. The 2001 season was a very disappointing one for all concerned at Old Trafford but with Mike Watkinson installed as the county's new coach, hopefully the near misses of recent years can be turned into Lancashire's first outright Championship success since 1934.

Though the county's fortunes in the post-war years have been mixed, Lancashire have produced many outstanding cricketers. I hope this book captures the character of some of them.

Dean P. Hayes
Pembrokeshire
March 2002

Paul Allott

Born: 14 September 1956, Altrincham, Cheshire
County debut: Lancashire v Gloucestershire at Bristol, 1978

- His best return for Lancashire was 8 for 48 v Northamptonshire at Northampton in 1981.
- He appeared in 13 Tests for England. His best figures were 6 for 61 v the West Indies at Headingley in 1984.
- He shared with Bob Willis in a record England tenth-wicket stand of 70 v India at Lord's in 1982, though his highest Test score was 52 not out v Australia at Old Trafford in 1981.

LANCASHIRE RECORD	
BATTING	
M	205
I	222
NO	52
Runs	2,877
HSc	88
Av	16.92
100	–
50	8
BOWLING	
Runs	13,434
Wkts	549
Av	24.46
Best	8–48
5w	24
10w	–

PAUL ALLOTT proved to be a fine servant to Lancashire despite suffering niggling injuries throughout his time with the county club.

He was educated at Altrincham Grammar School where his talent as a cricketer was first recognised and where he was considered as a player for the future. From school he moved into the England Schools Cricket Association Under-19 side, bowling big in-swingers. He toured the Caribbean in 1976 with the young side which included Mike Gatting and David Gower. This was the year in which he represented Cheshire in the Minor Counties League and a year later he made his debut for the Lancashire 2nd XI.

Paul Allott attended Durham University where fellow Lancashire players Graeme Fowler and Gehan Mendis were also studying. It is little wonder that Durham won the UAU Championship.

One of the most economical and accurate bowlers in limited-overs competitions, he could always be relied upon to produce a perfect off-stump line. His first match for Lancashire was in the Benson & Hedges Cup, his second in the John Player Sunday League, while his first game in the County Championship was against Gloucestershire at Bristol. Allott went out to Tasmania with Jack Simmons and on the slow wickets he was forced to concentrate all the more on line and length.

He was in the Lancashire side when Michael Holding made his county debut against Northamptonshire in 1981. Allott produced the best figures of his career, taking 8 for 48, and said at the time: 'Batsmen obviously aren't going to take chances against him, so they'll take chances against me' – a typically modest approach from a man who was quiet, reserved and softly spoken off the field but ready to fight on it. That season Allott took 75 wickets for Lancashire and was awarded his county cap. His performances, which included 6 for 105 against Yorkshire at old Trafford and 5 for 94 against Surrey at The Oval, along with his career-best figures in the Northamptonshire match, led to him being selected by England for the Old Trafford Test against Australia. Here he excelled with the bat and scored an unbeaten 52.

Allott appeared for England at Test level on 13 occasions. In 1982 he shared with Bob Willis in a record England tenth-wicket stand of 70 against India at Lord's, while his best figures with the ball were 6 for 61 against the West Indies at Headingley in 1984.

His high action and strong build brought him a number of consistent performances at county level including 7 for 42 against Kent at Maidstone in 1987. Then in 1988 he took 67 wickets, the most for the county, at an average of 20.56 runs apiece and a best of 6 for 59 against Essex

(LEP)

at Southend. In the Refuge Assurance Cup he won the man-of-the-match award in the semi-final against Gloucestershire for his performance with both bat and ball.

The following season in the NatWest Trophy match against Gloucestershire at Bristol he took 4 for 31 and was again named man-of-the-match after hitting a six to win the match. He also hit a six to win the Sunday League title in the match against Surrey at Old Trafford. Yet for all his match-winning performances for the county, he failed to score a century – 88 against Hampshire at Southampton in 1987 was his top score.

After taking only 18 wickets in 13 Britannic Assurance Championship matches in 1990 Paul Allott lost around 2 stone during the close season. Team-mates and opponents now detected an extra bit of zip in his bowling.

Playing his last season for the county in 1991, Paul Allott took 549 wickets at 24.46 runs each, a figure he would have exceeded if injuries had not deprived him of more appearances.

(LEP)

Michael Atherton

Born: 23 March 1968, Failsworth, Manchester
County debut: Lancashire v Warwickshire at Southport, 1987

- He was voted Young Cricketer of the Year and named as one of *Wisden*'s Five Cricketers of the Year in 1990.
- He scored 29 centuries for Lancashire with a highest of 268 not out v Glamorgan at Blackpool in 1998.
- He was made an OBE in 1997.
- He appeared in 115 Tests for England, scoring 7,728 runs at an average of 37.69 and a highest score of 185 not out v South Africa at Johannesburg in November 1995.
- He captained England a record 53 times.

LANCASHIRE RECORD

BATTING

M	151
I	252
NO	29
Runs	9,904
HSc	268*
Av	44.41
100	29
50	40

BOWLING

Runs	2,359
Wkts	61
Av	38.67
Best	6–78
5w	3
10w	–

EDUCATED at Manchester Grammar School and Cambridge University, where he excelled as a player and captain, Michael Atherton made his Test debut at 21 and impressed with his technique, temperament and composure at the crease.

In the summer the young Atherton would spend hours watching his father playing at the long-time family club, Woodhouses, in the Lancashire and Cheshire League. That's where cricket entered Michael Atherton's soul – there and at Briscoe Lane Primary School where the school's zest for the game won a number of local cups.

At Manchester Grammar School he smashed batting records and was in charge of the team at the age of 15. Older boys were happy to acknowledge his greater skill and knowledge of the game. At 16 he captained the England Under-19s, which reinforced the suspicion at the time that he would one day lead England through the Long Room at Lord's.

His career choice was confirmed after an unbeaten 73 as a freshman for Cambridge University against a rampant Essex attack. Cambridge had been reduced to 20 for 7 before Atherton worked his miracle. Captain of Cambridge, where he hit three centuries and a highest of 151 not out against Middlesex at Fenner's, he also led the Combined Universities on their enterprising giant-killing run in the Benson & Hedges Cup in 1989.

It is as a batsman that Atherton has made the greatest impact since making his Lancashire debut against Warwickshire at Southport in 1987. In scoring 1,193 first-class runs that summer he became the first batsman to make over 1,000 runs in a debut season since Paul Parker, another Cambridge man, in 1976.

He scored his maiden century for Lancashire against Sussex at Hove in 1988, when he made 152 not out. He finished the season with 456 runs and topped the Lancashire batting averages. In 1989 he was awarded his county cap and selected to play for England in two Tests against Australia, scoring 47 at Trent Bridge. At the end of the season he was chosen as vice-captain for the England 'A' team tour to Kenya and Zimbabwe, where his contribution to planning and strategy confirmed him as a ready-made successor to Graham Gooch as England's captain.

Atherton continued to score runs by the ton for Lancashire and he trod in some famous footprints at Trent Bridge in June 1990 to become, at 22, the youngest Englishman to make a Test hundred since the 21-year-old David Gower achieved the feat in India in 1978. That summer was also his first full season with Lancashire. No one at Old Trafford did more to lead

(LEP)

Lancashire's assault on the Britannic Championship, Benson & Hedges Cup and Refuge Assurance League. Atherton and Fairbrother followed their huge partnership of 364 against Surrey at The Oval with many other century stands, including the one which hoisted Lancashire into the Benson & Hedges final at Lord's. Atherton – all composure – and his Test colleague Fairbrother blitzed the Somerset attack in the semi-final in a third-wicket partnership of 115 runs in just 18 overs. Atherton ended the summer of 1990 with 1,170 runs at an average of 78.00.

(LEP)

In his early days with the county, Atherton was a wily leg-spinner and in 1990 produced his best figures with 6 for 78 against Nottinghamshire at Trent Bridge. His highest score for Lancashire was the unbeaten 268 against Glamorgan at Blackpool in 1998. Atherton also hit hundreds in each of the limited-overs competitions, with bests of 115 against Derbyshire in the NatWest Trophy of 1996; 121 not out against Durham in the Benson & Hedges Cup of 1996; and 111 against Essex in the Sunday League of 1990. He also hit 127 for England in a one-day international.

In 1993 Atherton followed Percy Chapman, Gubby Allen, Peter May, Ted Dexter, Mike Brearley and others from the fields of Fenner's to the tenancy of the captain's locker in the England dressing room.

Atherton's 'flawless' technique was still vulnerable against bowling of the highest class but his dogged determination – he didn't like getting out – and his remarkable powers of concentration coupled with nimble footwork took him into positions to play shots all round the wicket – a priceless gift for an opening batsman hoping not to get bogged down against tight bowling.

Often the springboard for many England innings but not always supported by his colleagues, Atherton went on to score 7,728 runs for his country at 37.69 with 16 centuries and 43 scores of more than 50. His highest score was his mammoth innings of 185 not out against South Africa at Johannesburg in November 1995. Atherton, who captained England a record 53 times and played in 63 consecutive Tests, made his 100th appearance at Test level against the West Indies at Old Trafford in 2000. After appearing in 2001's Ashes series against Australia, Atherton, who had played in 115 Tests, announced his retirement from the international scene. A few days later came his decision to leave Lancashire and take up a position with the media.

When he was interviewed in 1990, his first full season with the county, Atherton said: 'My only ambition is to captain Lancashire, and that when I am one of the senior players at Old Trafford.' Sadly, it was not to be.

Bob Barber

Born: 26 September 1935, Withington, Manchester
County debut: Lancashire v Glamorgan at Old Trafford, 1954

- He scored seven centuries for Lancashire with a highest of 175 v Kent at Folkestone in 1961.
- His best bowling for Lancashire was 7 for 35 v Derbyshire at Chesterfield in 1960.
- He captained Lancashire in seasons 1960 and 1961.
- With Lancashire team-mate Geoff Pullar, he shared in a record England opening partnership of 198 v Pakistan in Dacca in 1961/2.
- He scored 185 in 296 minutes off 255 balls at Sydney – the highest individual England score on the first day of a Test v Australia in 1965/6.
- He performed the hat-trick for Warwickshire v Glamorgan at Edgbaston in 1963.
- He appeared in 28 Tests for England.

LANCASHIRE RECORD

BATTING

M	155
I	264
NO	25
Runs	6,760
HSc	175
Av	28.28
100	7
50	29

BOWLING

Runs	4,768
Wkts	152
Av	31.36
Best	7–35
5w	3
10w	–

A SCHOOLBOY prodigy at Ruthin, where he did the double of 1,000 runs and 100 wickets, and a Cambridge University Blue, he became the second Light Blue captain of Lancashire in 1960.

He had made his debut for Lancashire in 1954 when he was still only 18 and midway between Ruthin College and Cambridge where he played for the university from 1954 to 1957. Most seasons he appeared occasionally at Old Trafford during his vacations from Cambridge and was being groomed as the golden boy to succeed Cyril Washbrook as captain.

When the Lancashire Committee elected him captain in 1960, they also made the decision to isolate him from the rest of the team: the committee members preferred the amateur captain to be with them while the professional players kept to themselves. This was a pity and proved to be a big mistake.

Bob Barber (batting in the picture) was a fine cricketer but he seems to have had difficulty choosing whether to play right- or left-handed – he was an attacking left-handed batsman with a superb array of shots all round the wicket and a very talented leg-break bowler but right-handed! Add to this his excellence in the field, notably in the leg-trap, and you have a superb all-round cricketer.

Barber got off to a flying start as Lancashire captain. Two victories over Yorkshire in the season, the first time since 1893 that Lancashire had achieved that feat, coupled with 13 other wins placed the county top of the table with just six games to go. However, the red rose side lost four and won none of their last six fixtures to finish in second place in the County Championship to Yorkshire. It was the second time since the war that Lancashire had ended the season as runners-up.

The captain seemed to be blamed for this disappointing end to the 1960 season, especially by members. Controversy seemed to follow him. In the match against Kent he had severely criticised Colin Cowdrey's leadership in Kent's successful effort to avoid defeat. The Lancashire Committee felt obliged to disassociate themselves publicly from Barber's remarks. There were a couple of occasions when Barber suffered from the committee's interference: Peter Marner was sent home after refusing to wear his blazer at lunch during the Kent match and Ken Higgs also had to leave because the committee thought he was too tired. At the end of Barber's first year as captain, Alan Wharton, his right-hand man, was effectively dismissed. After being offered the second team captaincy he was left with

(LEP)

little alternative but to resign. Barber again had no say in the matter and again felt completely isolated.

In 1961 the team finished in thirteenth place, the lowest-ever position in the county's history. The outstanding result of that otherwise disappointing summer came at Worksop where they beat Nottinghamshire by scoring 372 for 4 in five hours, including a magnificent century from Barber. The club's fade out towards the end of the previous season gave the committee a ready-made scapegoat in Bob Barber and they issued a statement in October 1961 explaining that they felt the pressures of captaincy had held him back as a player, also citing his reluctance to bowl himself. They had decided not to ask him to lead the club in 1962.

He played one more season under Joe Blackledge and then left Lancashire after nine seasons and 155 matches, during which he had scored 6,760 runs and captured 152 wickets. By this time he had played in nine Test matches, scoring 347 runs with a highest of 86 against Pakistan at Dacca and taking 15 wickets.

He had felt stifled at Old Trafford and moved on to Warwickshire, determined to express himself. At Edgbaston caution gave way to attack and he became one of the most attractive left-handed batsmen in the country. Opening the innings, he began to force the pace right from the outset. He played in 124 matches for Warwickshire in seven years and during those seasons scored 5,978 runs including nine centuries. One of them was a brilliant innings against the West Indies and another came before lunch on the first day against the Australians. He also captured 197 wickets at 24.64 with his leg-spin. Barber played in 19 more Test matches, ending with a batting average of 35.59. His appearances included an innings of 185 at Sydney – one of the greatest in Ashes history.

There was no doubt about it: Bob Barber was an individualist. He conformed to no pattern and was seen by some as an unorthodox player with a mind and temperament all his own. In the second Test of the 1964/5 South African tour, he had made 97 out of the first 146. Though within a fraction of his century, Barber went up to his partner, Ted Dexter, and said: 'Right six or out!' 'Don't be so bloody stupid,' said Dexter. 'I mean it,' replied Barber. Off-spinner Seymour was bowling at the time. Barber advanced to hit him straight, allowed for spin that was not there and deflected the delivery on to his wicket. He was not disappointed that he hadn't reached his hundred. He had gambled and lost.

Bob Barber was an adventurous cricketer and even after retirement the spirit was still there: he took part in an arduous expedition to the Himalayas.

Bob Berry

Born: 29 January 1926, Gorton, Manchester
County debut: Lancashire v Kent at Old Trafford, 1948

- He took all 10 wickets in an innings v Worcestershire at Blackpool in 1953, finishing with 10 for 102 and match figures of 14 for 125.
- He repeated these match figures of 14 for 125 v Somerset at Old Trafford in 1953, a season in which he took 98 wickets at 18.97 runs apiece.
- He appeared in two Tests for England, taking 5 for 63 and 4 for 53 on his debut v West Indies at Old Trafford in 1950.
- He was the first cricketer to be capped by three counties.

LANCASHIRE RECORD

BATTING

M	93
I	85
NO	34
Runs	427
HSc	27*
Av	8.37
100	–
50	–

BOWLING

Runs	5,900
Wkts	259
Av	22.77
Best	10–102
5w	13
10w	2

A LEFT-ARM spinner, Bob Berry played in 93 matches for Lancashire and would have appeared in many more but for the competition provided by Malcolm Hilton. He outshone Hilton in a couple of seasons, especially 1953 when he took 98 wickets at 18.97 runs each, including all ten for 102 against Worcestershire at Blackpool, only the third time in the county's history that this feat had been achieved.

The first county cricketer to be capped by three counties, Bob Berry's career started with Denton St Lawrence. He then moved on to Longsight before a successful trial took him to Lancashire for the 1948 season. He joined a Lancashire squad in which competition for the spin-bowling places was fierce: alongside Hilton and Berry was Roy Tattersall. However, Berry won a place and on occasions even opened the bowling with either Statham or Wharton. He was rewarded with his county cap during the 1950 Roses match at Sheffield.

His first England cap also came in 1950 when he was picked for the first Test against the West Indies at Old Trafford. Receiving a warm welcome from the home crowd, he took 5 for 63 and 4 for 53. His wickets included Clyde Walcott (twice) and Frank Worrell. England won by 202 runs and went to Lord's in high spirits. Alas they were beaten by 326 runs and Bob Berry's 0 for 45 and 0 for 67 meant he was left out for the remaining Tests. Others lost their places too.

He was invited to tour Australia with Freddie Brown's 1950/1 team but because he wasn't a great spinner of the ball, he did not play in any of the Tests. However, his good humour made him an important and popular member of the touring party.

Berry took all ten Worcestershire wickets in the match at Blackpool in July 1953. With Tattersall and Statham operating at the other end, it was amazing that he should dismiss the entire Worcestershire team. Lancashire, with a first-innings lead of 74, had closed their second innings at 262 for 8 declared. Berry took two early wickets bowling over the wicket, but then discovered some rough created by Alan Wharton just outside the leg stump and changed to bowling round the wicket. The visitors looked well beaten at 153 for 5 but Bob Broadbent and Richard Devereux put on 104 in 85 minutes before Berry separated them. The next four wickets fell to Berry and Lancashire won a great match by only 18 runs after seven minutes of the extra half-hour. Jack Ikin's four catches made an important contribution to Berry's piece of history-making. He had wheeled away for 36.2 unbroken overs to finish with 10 for 102 (14 for 125 in the match).

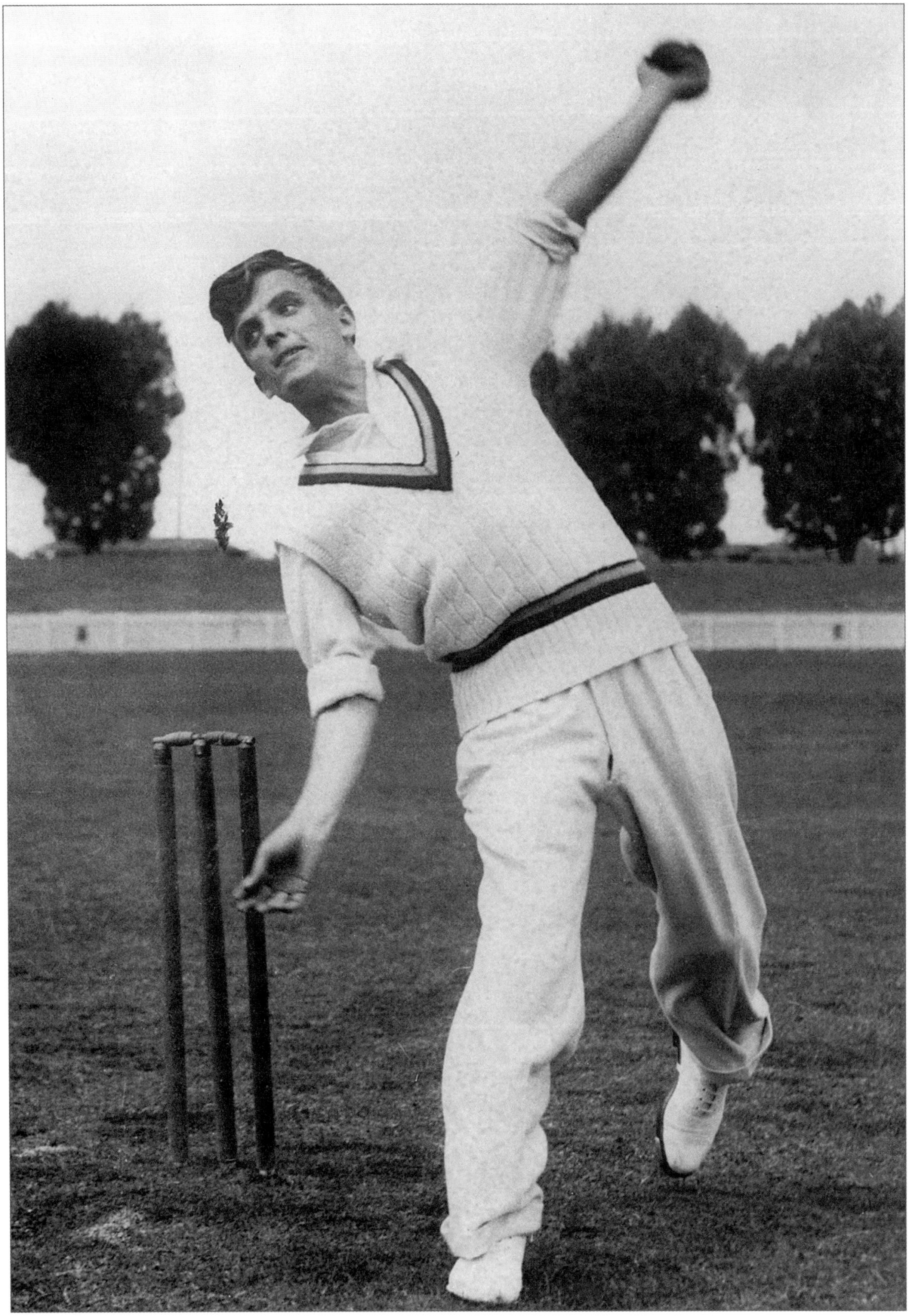

(LEP)

After four more seasons with Lancashire and a total of 259 first-class wickets, Berry asked for his release when he found himself in and out of the team. Worcestershire, obviously remembering that 10 for 102, quickly signed him and he went on to take 250 wickets for them, including 5 for 65 on his debut against the 1955 South Africans.

Berry was hurt in a bus accident on the way to the ground in 1958 and after his recovery found that Worcestershire were developing a new left-arm bowler, Doug Slade. He wrote to other counties asking if they required a bowler of his type and Derbyshire, who had only the off-spinner Edwin Smith, responded. At Derbyshire he took another 97 first-class wickets towards his final total of 703. Perhaps more importantly for a bowler whose career batting average was 7.58, he also made his top score of 40.

Berry's county career finished in 1962 and he became a professional with a Bass Brewery team in the North Staffordshire League. He played weekends and coached on Tuesdays and Thursdays. To augment his pay, Bass offered him an office job. But Berry decided office work was not for him and became a well-respected publican for the Bass Brewery at the Black Bull in Mansfield, where he also established a good reputation as a pigeon breeder.

Jack Bond

Born: 6 May 1932, Kearsley, Bolton
County debut: Lancashire v Surrey at Old Trafford, 1955

- He scored 14 centuries for Lancashire with a highest of 157 v Hampshire at Old Trafford in 1962.
- He captained Lancashire from 1968 to 1972, leading the side to the John Player League in 1969 and 1970 and the Gillette Cup in 1970, 1971 and 1972 as well as third place in the County Championship on two occasions.
- He was Lancashire's manager from 1980 to 1986.
- He was appointed a first-class umpire in 1988.

LANCASHIRE RECORD	
BATTING	
M	344
I	522
NO	76
Runs	11,867
HSc	157
Av	26.60
100	14
50	53
BOWLING	
Runs	69
Wkts	0

JACK BOND came from a staunch Methodist family in Little Hulton, near Bolton, where his father was a cotton spinner and his mother ran the family fish and chip shop. Every Methodist church had a cricket team in which the secretary attended to the equipment and organised practice nets, and it was in this atmosphere of cleaning pads, oiling bats and sometimes making up the number in the team, that Jack learned his cricket.

He played in teams at Hulton East and Bolton schools, compensating for his lack of height and slight build with the tenacity of his batting and the safety of his catching. After school he joined Walkden in the Bolton League, averaging 44 in his only season before moving to Radcliffe, where Cec Pepper was the professional. Pepper gave Bond much encouragement and advice. The *Manchester Evening Chronicle* sponsored eight boys for special coaching at Old Trafford and Bond became one of them. Under the guidance of Stan Worthington, his winter work was impressive enough to secure a county appointment in 1955.

Lancashire were lavishly staffed at this time and success could be measured by selection for the second team. Making the county side was a dream for young players but Bond did get a couple of games that season. Making his debut against Surrey, he was dismissed by Lock and Laker for 0 and 1. Years later he was fully avenged, taking a century from both bowlers. In 1955 Lancashire spared little thought for Jack Bond, a player whose main asset was his loyalty to the club and a middle-order average of around 20, yet he was always a man who tried.

Bond scored the first of his 14 centuries in 1959 – 101 not out at Trent Bridge against Nottinghamshire. In 1961 he scored 1,701 runs including three centuries to earn his county cap. This was bettered in 1962 when he scored 2,125 runs with his career best of 157 against Hampshire at Old Trafford. A successor to Cyril Washbrook, Bond seemed to be establishing himself when West Indian paceman Wes Hall broke his wrist as he attempted to fend off a fearsome delivery in Lancashire's match against the tourists in 1963. It took Bond some time to recover his old form and for the next few seasons he was in and out of the side, frequently captaining the 2nd XI. His success in that role led to him acting as deputy captain on a number of occasions in 1967 when Brian Statham was not fit to play, and when the great bowler resigned the captaincy, Jack Bond was appointed in his place.

He inherited a side that contained several fine players who were consistently playing below their potential, a reflection of the conflict and dissension behind the scenes at Old Trafford. Bond realised the weaknesses in his team and crystallised his approach to remedy them with

(LEP)

two main objectives. Firstly, he stressed the importance of fielding and made it clear that he was not prepared to consider anyone for a place in the side who was not committed to all-out effort to improve in this crucial area of the game. He preached the gospel of physical fitness and his players were urged and encouraged by Bond's own example to keep themselves in good trim. Secondly, he emphasised the need for a more positive and assertive approach in Lancashire's cricket, a faster scoring rate, tight field placing and accurate bowling.

In the first season of Bond's leadership Lancashire rose to sixth place in the County Championship table. The resurgence had begun. Engineer and Lloyd joined the nucleus of a side now strong enough to restore Lancashire's fortunes. Under Bond the renaissance began. In 1969, the year of the competition's inception, Lancashire won the John Player League Championship and by their shrewd pacing of an innings, tight fielding and accurate bowling Bond and his men proved themselves masters of limited-overs cricket.

Having finished a disappointing fifteenth in the County Championship in 1969, Lancashire rose to third place the following season with double the number of batting bonus points. They also won the John Player League Championship for the second year in succession and the Gillette Cup for the first time. It was Lancashire's best season for years. Under Bond's positive leadership and tactful understanding his players had welded together into a formidable side.

The 1971 season was a little less successful. Third position was maintained in the County Championship but the John Player League title went to Worcestershire. However, it was in 1971's Gillette Cup that Lancashire won their proudest honours and captured the imagination of the public during a series of brilliant victories. In all of them the guiding influence and tactical flair of Jack Bond was conspicuous, never more so than in the semi-final against Gloucestershire at Old Trafford and in the final against Kent at Lord's. Kent were chasing a Lancashire score of 224 for 7 and initially had not fared too well, losing half their wickets for 105. Then Asif Iqbal took command of the innings and with four wickets and six overs remaining he brought Kent to within 28 runs of victory. It seemed impossible to set a field to contain him and while he remained at the wicket, a Kent win looked a distinct possibility. Asif had scored 89 and then came the moment that decided the match. Simmons was bowling to a strong on-side field and Asif made room to off-drive, hitting the ball cleanly and with telling force seemingly well wide of extra-cover. Bond, who was fielding there, seemed to hesitate, but he suddenly took off and plucked the ball out of the air. Incredibly, he held on to it as he fell, rolling over and over on the ground. It was a catch in a thousand. The remaining wickets fell for the addition of only three runs and Lancashire had won the match and retained the Gillette Cup.

In 1972 Jack Bond led Lancashire to their third successive Gillette Cup victory when they beat Warwickshire by four wickets in another memorable match. At the end of that season, feeling that his playing days were coming to an end, he announced his retirement and was appointed to the coaching staff. He later left to play as captain for Nottinghamshire for a year.

Since the mid-1970s, Bond has coached at King William College on the Isle of Man, been a Test selector, run a public house and been a first-class umpire. He also became manager of Lancashire, helping them win the Benson & Hedges Cup in 1984. When he left the impression remained that it was he who had put Lancashire cricket back on top.

Ken Cranston

Born: 20 October 1917, Aigburth, Liverpool
County debut: Lancashire v Oxford University at The Parks, 1947

- He scored two centuries for Lancashire with a highest of 155 not out v Hampshire at Bournemouth in 1947.
- His best bowling for Lancashire was 7 for 43 (10 for 82 in the match) v Surrey at The Oval in 1948.
- He captained Lancashire in 1947 and 1948 and in both his seasons with the county, he came close to achieving the double.
- He appeared in eight Tests for England, captaining them at Bridgetown in 1947/8.
- He ended South Africa's second innings in the match at Headingley in 1947 by taking four wickets in an over!

LANCASHIRE RECORD

BATTING
M	50
I	57
NO	9
Runs	1,928
HSc	155*
Av	40.16
100	2
50	14

BOWLING
Runs	3,267
Wkts	142
Av	23.00
Best	7–43
5w	10
10w	1

THOUGH he only spent two years in first-class cricket, Ken Cranston played in eight Test matches, toured the West Indies with MCC, captained England in a Test and took four wickets in an over against South Africa.

Born in Aigburth, about a mile from the ground Lancashire started playing at in 1881, his introduction to first-class cricket was unusual to say the least. He played his schoolboy cricket in Liverpool where he attended the Liverpool College and was a regular member of the 1st XI from 1930 to 1935. In 1934 he played for the Young Amateurs against the Young Professionals at Lord's and a year later he secured a place in the Public Schools XI against the Army. He also scored 289 in three hours for the touring Liverpool Pilgrims at Eastbourne. Cranston played for Lancashire's 2nd XI and scored a century against Yorkshire 2nd XI before turning out for Royal Navy, Combined Services and Club Cricket Conference sides during the Second World War.

When county cricket resumed after the hostilities, Jack Fallows was a rush appointment as Lancashire captain to get the county through the 1946 season. Yet despite his team winning 15 out of 26 matches, certain members of the committee were already looking round for Fallows' successor.

Ken Cranston was making a name for himself with both bat and ball for Neston in the Liverpool Competition and it was to the all-rounder that Lancashire turned. When asked to take on the role, Cranston had a difficult decision to make: he was in the process of resuming a career in dentistry, which he had given up a couple of years previously. However, he accepted the captaincy and though it was only for a period of two years, the county had acquired probably their finest all-rounder captain. In 1947 he guided Lancashire to third place in the County Championship.

After just 13 matches for Lancashire, Cranston was selected for England. In both his seasons with the county he came close to doing the double of 1,000 runs and 100 wickets. He hit two centuries and his highest score of 155 not out came in the tied match with Hampshire at Bournemouth. Yet when asked to name his most memorable match, Cranston cited the county game against the Australians in which his role was negligible. In this match Malcolm Hilton dismissed Don Bradman twice in two days.

In the Test match at Headingley against South Africa in 1947 Cranston took four wickets in six balls and was chosen to tour West Indies during the following winter. On that tour of the

Caribbean he even captained England in one match when Gubby Allen was ill. In eight Tests he scored 209 runs at 14.92 and captured 18 wickets at 25.61 runs apiece.

In 1948 Lancashire slipped to fifth place and while Ken Cranston continued to enjoy his cricket tremendously, he was committed to dentistry and resigned at the end of the season. He was pressed to stay on, but his mind was made up. In just two years, Cranston had stamped his name on the game of cricket as a fine all-rounder.

He did not play for Lancashire again but was happy to take part in the occasional game for the Foresters and MCC. It was for MCC in the 1949 Scarborough Festival that he recorded his highest-ever score of 156 not out against Yorkshire.

Cranston's record for Lancashire in the two years he played was quite exceptional. He scored 1,928 runs at an average of 40.16 and took 142 wickets at a cost of just 23.00 runs each. It was a sad day for Lancashire cricket when this most amiable of men went back to extracting teeth.

John Crawley

Born: 21 September 1971, Maldon, Essex
County debut: Lancashire v Zimbabwe at Old Trafford, 1990

- He scored 182 and 108 in the match against Glamorgan at Old Trafford in 1995.
- His highest score of 281 not out was made against Somerset at Southport in 1994. He also scored 250 v Nottinghamshire at Trent Bridge in the same season, ending the summer with 1,472 runs at an average of 58.88.
- He was voted Young Cricketer of the Year in 1994.
- He has appeared in 29 Tests for England with a highest score of 156 not out v Sri Lanka at The Oval in 1998.
- He captained Lancashire from 1999 to 2001, leading the county to the CGU Division One (National League) Championship and runners-up spot in the County Championship in 1999 and 2000.

LANCASHIRE RECORD	
BATTING	
M	138
I	221
NO	15
Runs	10,542
HSc	281*
Av	51.17
100	31
50	51
BOWLING	
Runs	187
Wkts	1
Av	187.00
Best	1–90
5w	–
10w	–

WHEN JOHN CRAWLEY arrived at Cambridge University in 1990 he came with a reputation, and a reputation added to by several commentators who predicted an England place sooner rather than later. However, those expecting brilliance were disappointed as consistency rather than heavy scoring was the hallmark of his three seasons at Fenner's.

In 1990 he had scored 76 for Lancashire on his debut against the Zimbabweans at Old Trafford. Then on his debut for Cambridge against Lancashire in 1991 he reached 83. That summer Crawley made 66 and 59 not out in the annual Varsity match at Lord's and scored his first hundred for Lancashire, 130 against Surrey at Old Trafford.

Appointed Cambridge University captain in 1992, he scored a magnificent unbeaten 106 in the 147th Varsity match to lead his side to victory by seven wickets. Despite, by his own admission, a certain defensiveness in his game, 1992 proved a surprisingly successful year for a supposedly weak Cambridge XI and they also achieved a victory over Kent. That summer Crawley played in seven games for Lancashire and scored 172 against Surrey at Lytham.

In 1993 Crawley topped the Cambridge batting averages for the third year in succession, scoring 828 runs for an average of 69.00. He hit his highest score for the University – 187 not out in the match against Sussex at Hove. He also played in ten games for Lancashire in 1993 and appeared for England 'A' against Essex. By the time he left Fenner's he had scored 1,988 runs at an average of 49.70.

In 1994, his first full season at Old Trafford, Crawley topped the Lancashire batting averages, scoring 1,300 runs at an average of 61.90, and hit the highest score of his career, 281 not out against Somerset at Southport. His impressive performances led to his first Test cap which came against South Africa at Lord's and though he did not play to his potential in the three matches that followed, he was chosen to tour Australia in the winter of 1994/5. Despite a fighting innings of 72 at Sydney in the third Test and 71 in the fourth at Adelaide where England won, Crawley was fair game for hoary jibes when he had a shade too much 'power behind the saddle'. At 6ft 1in tall and 14st 7lb, Crawley was hardly Bunteresque, but he was carrying a surplus. There were those who regarded this as evidence of a lack of dedication and after a 'pair' in the final Test at Perth in February 1995 he needed to do

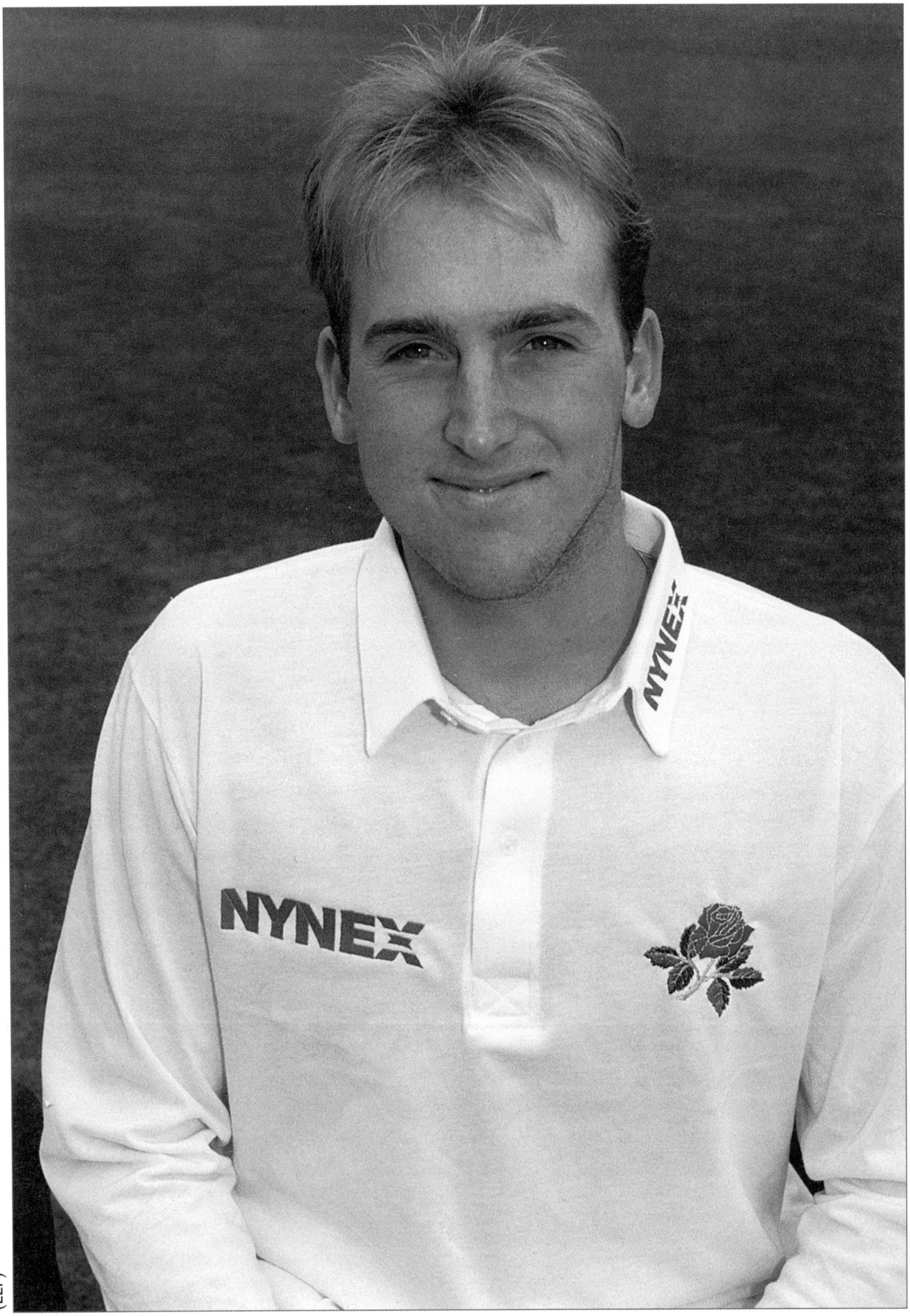

(LEP)

something about it. A friend who used to be a marathon runner helped him to emerge from weeks of exercise in a London fitness centre to confront those who had claimed he was too bulky, cumbersome and slow in the field.

Crawley topped the Lancashire batting averages again in 1995, scoring 1,203 runs at 52.30. In the match against Glamorgan at Old Trafford, he made 182 and 108 to register a hundred in each innings of the match. In 1996 he scored 904 runs at 53.17, the first season that he failed to score 1,000 runs for the county, but Crawley had by now forced himself into the England team on a regular basis. In the third and final Test against Pakistan at The Oval, he scored a polished and composed maiden Test century, yet, surprisingly for a good fielder and good one-day player, he was left out of the Texaco Trophy matches. Since then he has appeared in 29 Tests for England, scoring 1,329 runs at an average of 31.64 and a highest score of 156 not out against Sri Lanka at The Oval in 1998.

For Lancashire he has continued to impress in both County Championship and one-day matches, and when the red rose county won the NatWest Trophy in 1996, he top-scored with a fighting 66 – an exceptional, skilful effort in the mischievous conditions. He topped Lancashire's batting averages in 1997 and 1998, the latter season scoring 1,681 runs at 70.04 with seven centuries.

Appointed captain for the start of the 1999 season, Crawley led Lancashire to success in the CGU National League Division One and to second place in the County Championship, a position they achieved again in 2000. In 2001 he passed the milestone of 10,000 first-class runs for Lancashire during his innings of 73 in the Roses match at Headingley.

John Crawley is that rare breed of talented cricketer whose average of 51.17 places him at the top of the all-time list of batsmen. Surprisingly, he was relieved of the captaincy in the autumn of 2001. Following the appointment of wicket-keeper Warren Hegg as county captain for 2002, Crawley made it clear that he wished to be released from his contract, which still has three seasons to run. England and Wales Cricket Board rules state that he cannot be signed in the interim by another county without Lancashire's consent. Crawley has decided to seek advice from lawyers on whether he has a case against Lancashire and the ECB for restraint of trade. 'There are irreconcilable differences between Lancashire and myself,' he said. 'I feel I have been badly treated and because of this I do not feel I can ever represent Lancashire again.' Crawley is now playing for Hampshire and represented England in the first Test against Sri Lanka in 2002.

Geoff Edrich

Born: 13 July 1918, Lingwood, Norfolk
County debut: Lancashire v Gloucestershire at Gloucester 1946

LANCASHIRE RECORD	
BATTING	
M	322
I	479
NO	55
Runs	14730
HSc	167*
Av	34.74
100	24
50	76
BOWLING	
Runs	199
Wkts	2
Av	99.50
Best	1-19
5w	–
10w	–

- He scored 1,000 runs in a season on eight occasions with a best of 1,977 at 41.18 in 1952.
- He scored 24 centuries for Lancashire with a highest of 167 not out v Nottinghamshire at Trent Bridge in 1954.
- A fine slip fielder, he held 322 catches for Lancashire.

ONE OF FOUR first-class cricketing brothers, Geoff Edrich was born at Lingwood, Norfolk, the son of William, a keen Norfolk club cricketer who kept wicket and scored his first hundred when he was 40.

Geoff appeared for his home county before the outbreak of the Second World War, impressing with his attractive batting and brilliant fielding close to the wicket. During the hostilities he fought against the Japanese and was held prisoner of war for three-and-a-half years before being freed in August 1945, by which time he weighed just 6½ stone.

He had been approached by Hampshire in 1940, but in 1946 he was recommended to Lancashire, who signed him and his brother Eric on the basis of their pre-war reputations with Norfolk.

Eric only played until 1948, scoring 854 runs at an average of 23.72 including two centuries against Warwickshire and Yorkshire in his final season. Geoff continued to appear for Lancashire until 1958, scoring 14,730 runs at an average of 34.74 and reaching 1,000 runs in a season eight times. His best seasons were 1951 when he scored 1,693 runs at an average of 43.41 and 1952 when he failed by just 23 runs to reach 2,000 and averaged 41.18.

During 1951 Lancashire had to dig deep into their reserve strength when they met Hampshire at Aigburth: five of their players – Hilton, Howard, Ikin, Statham and Tattersall – were appearing in the Gentlemen v Players match at Lord's. However, Lancashire still won by an innings with Edrich scoring 155, the highest of his seven centuries that season.

Though he scored 24 centuries for Lancashire, one of Edrich's finest innings came in the match against Northamptonshire at Old Trafford. The visitors won a low-scoring game on a very difficult pitch by one wicket. Edrich scored 81 not out in Lancashire's second innings total of 141. The highest of his centuries was an unbeaten 167 against Nottinghamshire at Trent Bridge in 1954.

A member of the 1953/4 Commonwealth team to India, he scored 104 against Hyderabad and 112 against the Combined Universities at Bangalore.

A principled and steadfast man, Geoff Edrich had an altercation with authority in his early days with the county. Playing away from home, the team were invited to a Saturday night dance. Even though there was no cricket on Sundays then, Dick Pollard started to line up the players at midnight to check all of them were returning to the hotel. Edrich told him in no uncertain terms that he had been a prisoner of war for three-and-a-half years and nobody was going to tell him how to spend his Saturday nights!

In 1956 when Washbrook was recalled to England, Edrich was given the opportunity of captaining the county. Six of the ten matches in which he led the side were won. One of them created an unusual record when Lancashire beat Leicestershire at Old Trafford without losing a wicket, Edrich declaring early on the final day. Another piece of history was made in the following match when Edrich declared after only one ball of the second innings. At the time this was the shortest innings in history but for once his courageous tactics did not work: Nottinghamshire were given two hours to score 98 for victory and ended on 93 for 7.

Edrich later captained the 2nd XI with good sense and pragmatic judgement but lost the position when, characteristically, he refused to inform on younger members of his side after a silly prank in a hotel. He left Lancashire in 1958 to play Minor Counties cricket for Cumberland and pursue a life in schools coaching.

Farokh Engineer

Born: 25 February 1938, Bombay, India
County debut: Lancashire v Kent at Canterbury, 1968

- He helped to dismiss 464 batsmen (429 caught and 35 stumped).
- His best season behind the stumps was 1970 when he helped to dismiss 91 batsmen (86 caught and 5 stumped).
- He scored four centuries for Lancashire with a highest of 141 v Derbyshire at Buxton in 1971.
- He helped dismiss eight batsmen in a match for Lancashire on four occasions.
- He appeared in 46 Tests for India, his highest score being 121 v England at Bombay in 1972/3.
- His highest-ever score was 192 for a World XI v Combined XI at Hobart in 1972-72.

LANCASHIRE RECORD

BATTING

M	175
I	262
NO	39
Runs	5942
HSc	141
Av	26.64
100	4
50	25

BOWLING

Runs	10
Wkts	0

BORN IN BOMBAY of Parsee parents, Farokh Engineer was taught by the Jesuit priests of the Don Bosco school. In their wisdom the fathers decreed that the boys should play soccer and learn tennis, hockey and swimming but not cricket. Farokh played all the sports and featured as goalkeeper in the soccer side, playing with the same enthusiasm he showed in his cricket career.

The encouragement for Engineer's cricket came from his parents and from the University at Bombay where he read advanced economics and commerce before taking a degree and specialising in accountancy and auditing. While at university he made his debut in representative cricket, playing for Combined Universities against the West Indies in 1958/9. Thereafter he was a feature of Indian cricket, playing for Bombay in the Ranji Trophy, for West Zone in the Duleep Trophy and for India in Test cricket in every cricketing country except South Africa.

He toured England for the first time in 1967 with the Nawab of Pataudi's side and joined Lancashire on an immediate registration a year later. He made his first appearance for the county against Kent at Canterbury but that first season in English cricket was disappointing. Engineer rarely demonstrated the batting qualities that had prompted the Lancashire Committee to engage him as a wicket-keeper/batsman.

It is conceivable that experimenting with his batting position did not help his form or confidence. He batted at No.5 in a Gillette Cup game at Trent Bridge early in the season and was run out for 10. At No.4 in the county game against Kent at Canterbury he was bowled for 15 in the first innings and caught at the wicket for 1 in the second. He went back to No.5 at The Oval only to be run out for 23; and was at No.4 again against Nottinghamshire but failed to score. Still at No.4 he was dismissed for 1 and 0 at Lord's. When Middlesex came to Old Trafford he was dropped in the order to No.7 and scored 7 and 10. Then somebody remembered that he had opened the batting for India in Test matches and that he once scored 50 in both innings in Australia, made 94 not out before lunch off the bowling of Hall, Griffiths and Sobers, and scored over 100 before lunch in the 1964/5 final of the Duleep Trophy.

When Lancashire played Sussex at Eastbourne he was called upon to open the innings but sadly there was no improvement. Then at Southport Derbyshire dismissed him for a single in each innings and at Cambridge he suffered the traumatic experience of hitting his own wicket. Apart from scoring 70 against Somerset at Old Trafford and 54 against Warwickshire at Aigburth, there was very little for members to enthuse about over Engineer's batting in 1967.

(LEP)

Behind the stumps he had 62 victims, but these figures did not appease the Lancashire supporters who had expected a batsman/wicket-keeper rather than a wicket-keeper/batsman.

Much better was to come: in 1969 he failed by only 48 runs to reach 1,000. Had he not missed four games through injury, he would almost certainly have achieved that distinction. He made his first century for the county, 103 not out against Glamorgan at Swansea, in 1969 and to show that his wicket-keeping was not being neglected, he took eight catches when Lancashire played Somerset at Taunton.

As a batsman Farokh Engineer was essentially a swashbuckler. Exciting and eccentric, he was vulnerable to almost any bowler in cricket who could turn an arm over, but on the other hand the best in the game were banged against the sightscreen or lifted into the tea tent when he was at his most destructive. One Sunday afternoon at Buxton he narrowly missed scoring the fastest fifty of the season in a John Player League game and this innings is still spoken of with awe in that Derbyshire spa town.

When Glamorgan visited Southport for a televised Sunday League game in 1969 they were quickly dismissed for 112. Lancashire won by nine wickets, with Engineer hitting 78 not out in flamboyant style. The Glamorgan opening bowler Ossie Wheatley was heard to say: 'I don't mind him charging, but I do wish he would let me set off first.'

As a wicket-keeper his great reflexes meant he would often take catches in front of first slip. He was also one of the few modern-day wicket-keepers who would stand right up to fast-medium bowlers. A friendly man, he would often exchange words with the batsman. But it wasn't just the opposition he would talk to and the topic of conversation was not always cricket. Engineer was adored by youngsters and before the start of a game he would encourage lads to bowl and field to him.

Farokh Engineer has probably done more than any other player to promote Indian cricket to world-class status, certainly more than any other player since the war and that includes Kapil Dev and Sunil Gavaskar. He represented India on 46 occasions, scoring 2,611 runs at an average of 31.08 and also recorded 82 dismissals (66 caught and 16 stumped). He hit centuries all around the world – Calcutta, Bombay, Perth, Brisbane and Swansea. Yet he had to wait until 1975 before he notched his one and only hundred at Old Trafford against Warwickshire. Farokh sacrificed his wicket many a time for the good of his side and there are not too many cricketers who will do that. The Roses match at Sheffield's Bramall Lane ground in 1969 was the scene of a performance which perhaps typifies the man. Engineer had scored 96 when he tried to reach his hundred by hitting a six. He lashed out to a ball bowled by Geoff Cope and gave a simple catch to mid-on. He walked back to the pavilion muttering something like: 'Rookie, you silly man! What makes you do these daft things?'

Neil Fairbrother

Born: 9 September 1963, Warrington
County debut: Lancashire v Kent at Old Trafford, 1982

- His best season in terms of runs scored was 1990 when he scored 1,681 runs at 80.04 and a best of 366 v Surrey at The Oval.
- He has scored 46 centuries for Lancashire.
- He scored exactly 1,000 runs in all competitions in May 1990 – County Championship 674, Refuge Assurance League 125 and Benson & Hedges Cup 201 runs.
- In 1991 he hit three hundreds in succession: 107 not out, 109 and 102 not out including the latter two in the match v Somerset at Taunton.
- He has appeared in ten Tests and 75 one-day internationals for England with a best score of 113 v West Indies at Lord's in a one-day match in 1991.

LANCASHIRE RECORD

BATTING

M	325
I	517
NO	72
Runs	19,197
HSc	366
Av	43.13
100	46
50	96

BOWLING

Runs	473
Wkts	7
Av	67.57
Best	2–91
5w	–
10w	–

IT IS HIGHLY appropriate that Neil Harvey Fairbrother should have developed into a nimble-footed left-handed middle-order batsman and outstandingly agile cover fielder like the Australian Test cricketer whose names he was given.

It was with Grappenhall, a Manchester Association side, that the young Fairbrother first came to the notice of Lancashire. He made his county debut against Kent at Old Trafford in 1982. He did not bat in that match, his debut innings coming the following season in the match against Warwickshire at Edgbaston. John Abrahams was captaining Lancashire in Clive Lloyd's absence and agreed with Warwickshire captain Bob Willis early in the day to close Lancashire's innings of 250, which was 146 in arrears, and thereby set up a victory chase. Fairbrother was on 94 when 250 was reached and Abrahams having given his word, would not go back on it. Willis could have given Fairbrother the deliveries necessary for him to reach a historic hundred but immediately turned on his heels at 250 and left the field, much to the disgust of a number of players and the indignation of supporters.

Since then Fairbrother has made 19,197 runs and 46 centuries. They include one triple century and four doubles for Lancashire. His highest score of 366 was made against Surrey at The Oval in 1990. It was a psychological breakthrough, giving Fairbrother the confidence of knowing that he was capable of playing a major innings at any time. His performance broke a number of records: the highest score by an Englishman in the twentieth century; the highest score at The Oval, beating Len Hutton's 364 not out; the highest score against

(LEP)

Surrey; and the highest by a player batting at No.4. He also became the first batsman to score 100 runs or more in all three sessions of a day's play and with Mike Atherton put on 364, a record for Lancashire's third-wicket partnership.

In May 1990, Fairbrother scored exactly 1,000 runs in all competitions – 674 in the County Championship, 125 in the Refuge Assurance League and 201 in the Benson & Hedges Cup. In 1991 he hit three hundreds in succession – 107 not out against Glamorgan at Aigburth and 109 and 102 not out against Somerset at Taunton.

Despite an unlucky and traumatic start to his Test career, where his first four Test appearances yielded only five runs, he fought back to play in a further six Tests with a highest score of 83 against India in Madras. He has played in 75 one-day internationals for England, scoring 2,092 runs at an average of 39.47, including a magnificent 113 against the West Indies at Lord's in 1991. He has also won two man-of-the-match awards.

In limited-overs games for Lancashire, he has scored five hundreds in the Sunday League with a best of 116 not out against Nottinghamshire at Trent Bridge in 1988 and the same top score of 116 not out against Scotland in the Benson & Hedges Cup. Fairbrother led the county in the Benson & Hedges Cup final of 1991 and the Refuge Assurance Cup final of the same year – Lancashire lost both matches to Worcestershire. He was officially appointed David Hughes' successor in September 1991.

At first his form wasn't affected by his new responsibilities and in 1992 his unbeaten 166 against Yorkshire propelled him to the top of the national batting averages. However, the summer of 1993 was a desperately unhappy one for Neil Fairbrother. His form was so diminished by the trials of leadership that he went into September without a first-class century to his name. Though he did score 110 against Northamptonshire at Old Trafford, he had seven times been out for nought and had seen his chances of another England tour all but disappear.

He stepped down from the captaincy after two seasons and in 1994 returned to something like his old form, hitting four centuries including 204 against Middlesex at Old Trafford. In 1995 his benefit realised £206,000 and this was the year he signed a new five-year contract with Lancashire. In 1996 Fairbrother was part of the Lancashire side that won both the NatWest Trophy and the Benson & Hedges Cup, and in the second of those competitions he top-scored in the final with an innings of 63, though it was Ian Austin with 4 for 21 who won the man-of-the-match award.

Over the next few seasons injuries hampered his progress somewhat but in 2000 and 2001 the amiable Fairbrother topped the Lancashire batting averages. In the course of the match against Northamptonshire at Old Trafford in August 2001 he passed 20,000 runs in first-class cricket.

Though now 38, Fairbrother remains, in the author's opinion, the county's best batsman in all forms of cricket.

Graeme Fowler

Born: 20 April 1957, Accrington
County debut: Lancashire v Derbyshire at Chesterfield, 1979

- He scored centuries – 126 and 128 not out – in each innings of the match against Warwickshire at Southport in 1982.
- He scored 29 centuries for Lancashire with a highest of 226 v Kent at Maidstone in 1984.
- He appeared in 21 Tests for England with a highest score of 201 v India in Madras in 1984/5.
- He scored 1,000 runs in a season on seven occasions with a best of 1,800 at 47.36 in 1987.
- He holds the Lancashire record for the highest innings in the Benson & Hedges Cup with 136 v Sussex at Old Trafford in 1991.
- He scored 100 in 46 minutes (in farcical circumstances against non-bowlers) for Lancashire v Leicestershire at Old Trafford in 1983 – including ten consecutive scoring strokes for six – a first-class world record. His first-wicket stand of 201 in 43 minutes with Steve O'Shaughnessy is the fastest on record lasting over 30 minutes.

LANCASHIRE RECORD

BATTING

M	234
I	395
NO	27
Runs	13,453
HSc	226
Av	36.55
100	29
50	65

BOWLING

Runs	312
Wkts	8
Av	39.00
Best	2–34
5w	–
10w	–

GRAEME FOWLER did not start to play cricket until he was twelve. While on a family holiday in Devon, his father got him to bat and back home, coaching lessons in the garden followed. Within three years, Fowler was the youngest batsman in the Lancashire League, where he first appeared for his home-town team, Accrington, and then Rawtenstall.

He played his first match for Lancashire 2nd XI at the age of 16 in 1973 and over the next couple of seasons represented the English Schools Cricket Association, MCC Schools and Young England – all this as a wicket-keeper/batsman. In 1976 he was the Lancashire Cricket Federation Young Cricketer of the Year. Like Paul Allott he attended Durham University and in 1978 he left as a qualified physical education teacher to join Lancashire on a full-time basis. His hopes were soon dashed, however, when he injured his foot in a car crash and was out of the game for several months.

He made his county debut against Derbyshire at Chesterfield in 1979 and the following season scored the first of his 29 centuries for Lancashire, an unbeaten 106 against Nottinghamshire at Old Trafford. He spent that winter in Australia, working as a groundsman and playing for the Scarborough Club in Perth. He admitted that the pace and bounce were initially too much for him, but he returned to Lancashire and, through being less committed to the front foot, scored 1,560 runs at an average of 40.00 and was awarded his county cap. He followed this with 1,246 runs at 42.96 in 1982 and 1,269 runs at 55.17 in 1983.

With the exception of his Test debut against Pakistan in 1982 where he top scored in the second innings with 86, the highlight of his career must have been his two centuries in the match against Warwickshire at Southport. The visitors declared on the first day at 523 for 4 with Humpage and Kallicharran sharing in a partnership of 470 in 293 minutes. Lancashire declared 109 behind after a century from Fowler in 109 minutes. Les McFarlane took a career-best return of 6 for 59 in Warwickshire's second innings to set up an astonishing win for Lancashire. Then Fowler scored an unbeaten 128 to go with his 126 in the first innings and established the unusual record of scoring two centuries in the same match while batting with the aid of a runner!

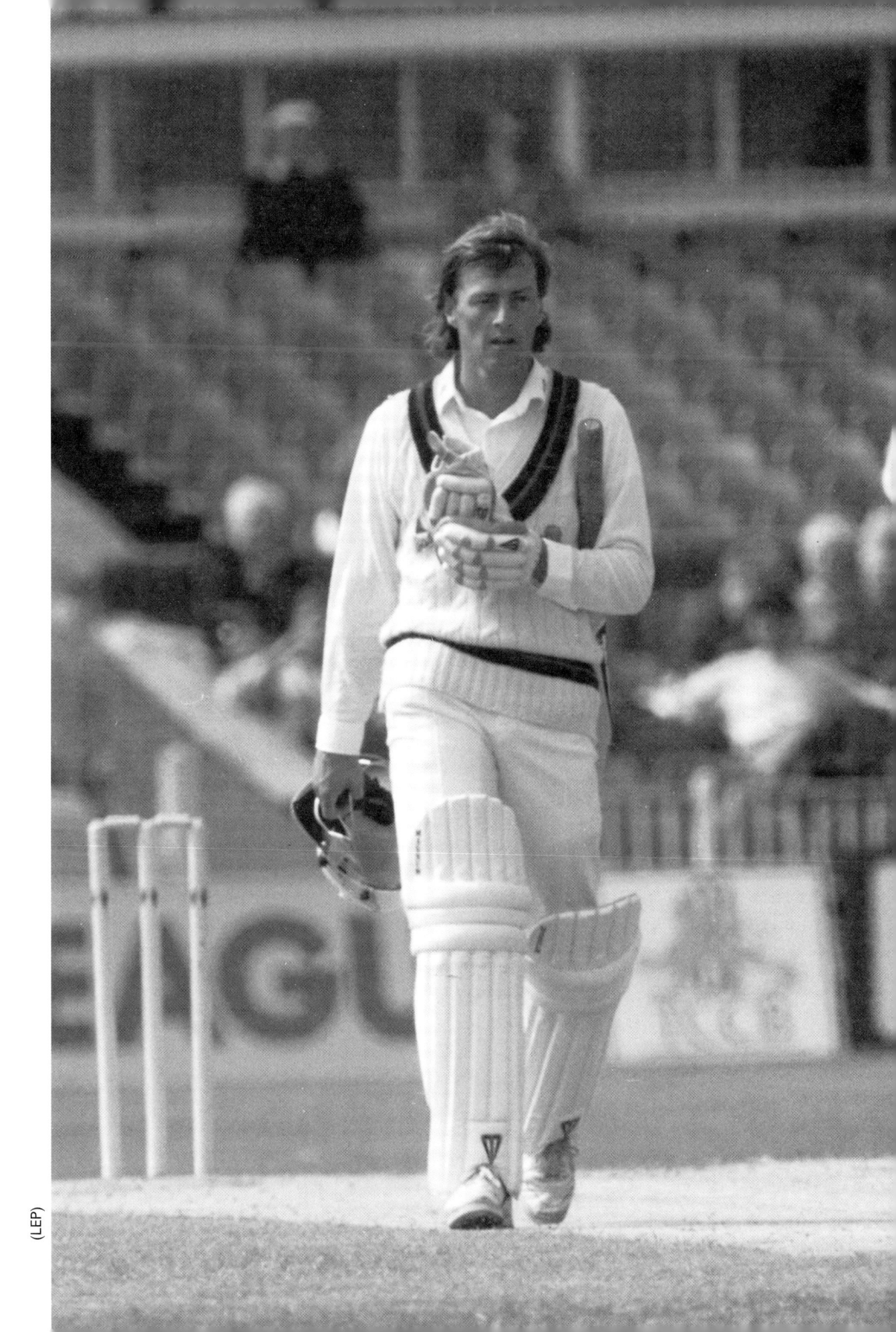

(LEP)

Fowler's excursion into Test cricket coincided exactly with the period of Graham Gooch's ban for touring South Africa. He hit his first Test century against New Zealand at The Oval in 1983, a season in which he scored a century against Leicestershire at Old Trafford in 46 minutes. His innings included ten consecutive scoring strokes for six – a first-class world record – as he and Steve O'Shaughnessy put on 201 in 43 minutes for the first wicket.

In 1984 he scored his second Test century, a fighting 106 against West Indies at Lord's, and hit the highest score of his career, 226 against Kent at Maidstone. Touring India in 1984/5, he became the first England player to score a Test double century in India when he made 201 at Madras. He followed this with 69 at Kanpur but was then dropped! In his 21 appearances for England he scored 1,307 runs at an average of 35.32.

A superb one-day player, he made 773 runs in the 1990 Sunday League (a record for Lancashire) despite suffering from a neck injury. During his playing career he scored five centuries and 4,853 runs in the Sunday League, a total second only to Clive Lloyd. He also hit two hundreds in the NatWest Trophy and holds the county record for the highest score in the Benson & Hedges Cup with a superb innings of 136 against Sussex at Old Trafford in 1991. His character, charm and ability – as well as his fallibility – brought him close to Lancashire supporters and was perhaps evident in the response to his record benefit of £152,885.

At the end of the 1992 season Fowler was released after scoring 13,453 runs at an average of 36.55. It came as no surprise and neither, once he decided to stay in the game, was his choice of new employer. Somerset had initially shown an interest but Durham were prepared to offer Fowler a two-year contract and a greater likelihood of regular first-team cricket. Although now aged 35, Fowler was very fit and added an edge to Durham's fielding. He didn't have too long to wait for a spot of nostalgia because Durham visited Old Trafford for their opening games in the Championship and Sunday League.

He played two seasons for Durham before leaving the first-class game. He was then based at Durham University's Cricket Centre of Excellence, set up with funds from the TCCB via the Cricket Foundation.

Tommy Greenhough

Born: 9 November 1931, Cronkeyshaw, Rochdale
County debut: Lancashire v Hampshire at Liverpool, 1951

- He took 100 wickets in a season on two occasions with a best of 119 at 17.85 in 1960.
- His best bowling for Lancashire was 7 for 56 v Worcestershire at New Road in 1964.
- He appeared for England in four Tests with a best performance of 5 for 35 v India at Lord's in 1959.

LANCASHIRE RECORD	
BATTING	
M	241
I	298
NO	79
Runs	1,868
HSc	76*
Av	8.52
100	–
50	1
BOWLING	
Runs	15,540
Wkts	707
Av	21.98
Best	7–56
5w	32
10w	5

LEG-SPINNER Tommy Greenhough spent 15 years at Old Trafford from 1951, taking 707 wickets at 21.98 runs apiece. He took over 100 wickets in two seasons, in spite of a succession of niggling injuries. Indeed, it was a miracle that he played the game at all. A year before his first-class debut in January 1950 he fell out of a loading bay at Edwards & Bryning's warehouse in Rochdale, smashing the metatarsals in both feet and thus severely jeopardising his future prospects in the game.

He grew up in the terraced streets of Cronkeyshaw and was spotted at the age of 14 by Levi Dearden, a stalwart of Fieldhouse Cricket Club in the Rochdale and District League, while bowling off-spinners and leg-spinners during the tea interval of a Wood Cup game at Rochdale. He developed essentially as an off-spinner, only accommodating the googly after watching a school friend who didn't even bowl regularly. In Greenhough's second season at Fieldhouse, Lancashire were alerted by the father of Len Hopwood, a league umpire. The Old Trafford coach, Harry Makepeace, was absolutely astounded to hear young Greenhough's credentials – 'I bowl all three sir, offers, leggies and googlies!' Borrowing something of Kent and England bowler Doug Wright's long bounding approach, Greenhough clasped the ball in cupped hands as if he were cradling a baby at arm's length before running to the wicket – it really was an extraordinary sight. Bowling with a fast action and speed through the air, Greenhough interspersed his leg-spinners with the occasional googly, a devastating proposition on a bouncy pitch.

He made his first-class debut for Lancashire in July 1951 in the match against Hampshire at Aigburth and his first wicket was that of Neville Rogers. He went on to play in 241 matches for Lancashire but in 1958 he was prepared to leave the county after constantly being left out on the soft pitches. Lancashire captain Cyril Washbrook intervened, telling Greenhough that as from the next season, wickets were to be covered and that he'd be in the first team right from the start.

However, he was affected by injuries. Damage to his hand resulting from striking his thigh in delivery restricted him and necessitated a wad of stockings stuffed into his pocket for a short period! Far more serious damage occurred when the affable Greenhough guested as deputy professional for Enfield against Church in a Lancashire League match. Attempting to take a fierce caught-and-bowled chance off Frank Worrell, he damaged a finger so severely that only the skill of the surgeons at Manchester Hospital prevented its removal.

Tommy Greenhough's Test debut came in 1959 against India at Trent Bridge. England made 422, then Peter May introduced Greenhough early. His 16-over spell yielded just 16 runs and the wicket of Contractor, the left-hander caught at long-leg by Ken Barrington off what was probably Greenhough's worst delivery. In the second Test at Lord's Greenhough played his part in helping dismiss India for 168 in their first innings by taking 5 for 12 in 31 balls, despite Godfrey Evans missing four possible stumpings within the space of 15 minutes. He followed this up with 2 for 48 off 23 overs and then decided he'd leave the game for a short while to try to eradicate his tendency of following through on to the pitch. Though he returned to the England side for the fifth Test at The Oval, where he recorded a match analysis of 4 for 83 in 56 overs, he never quite overcame the problem.

In that 1959 season of covered pitches Greenhough took 102 wickets at 23.53 apiece while 23 batsmen scored more than 2,000 runs. That really was a performance of a good bowler.

During England's tour of the Caribbean in 1959/60 Greenhough only appeared in six first-class fixtures. He claimed 21 wickets, more than anyone else bar Allen and Trueman. He started the tour well with 6 for 32 in the opening match against the Windward Islands in Grenada, defeating everyone with the googly. In the second match against Barbados he could not grip the ball properly due to perspiration, although he did remove Gary Sobers caught and bowled for 154.

Returning to Lancashire, he had a superb season in 1960 with 119 wickets at 17.85 runs apiece and displaced Ray Illingworth for the Test against South Africa at The Oval. It was Greenhough's final appearance at this level; he had taken 16 wickets at 22.31 runs apiece in his four Tests.

In 1961 Greenhough's progress was halted by yet another finger injury and in the following years, his feet became ever more troublesome, causing him to miss a good number of games. Cec Pepper suggested that Greenhough try a shorter approach to the wicket in an effort to improve his balance, but try as he might, Rochdale's only Test cricketer had lost his pace and bounce and in August 1966 he was dismissed without ceremony.

Ken Grieves

Born: 27 August 1925, Burwood, Sydney, Australia
Died: 3 January 1992
County debut: Lancashire v Sussex at Old Trafford, 1949

- He scored 26 centuries for Lancashire with a highest of 224 v Cambridge University at Fenner's in 1957.
- He scored 1,000 runs in a season on 13 occasions with a best of 2,253 at 41.72 in 1959.
- He holds the county record for the most catches in a career with 555, over 200 more than next-placed Archie MacLaren.
- He holds the record for the most catches in a season with 63 in 1950.
- He held eight catches in the match v Sussex at Old Trafford in 1951 including six in an innings.
- He captained Lancashire in 1963 and 1964.

LANCASHIRE RECORD

BATTING

M	452
I	696
NO	73
Runs	20,802
HSc	224
Av	33.39
100	26
50	129

BOWLING

Runs	6,769
Wkts	235
Av	28.80
Best	6–60
5w	8
10w	–

ONE OF LANCASHIRE'S outstanding all-round cricketers, Ken Grieves was born in Burwood, Sydney, and played his early cricket with the Petersham club which also produced such fine players as Sid Barnes, Cec Pepper, Bill Alley, Ernie Toshack and Bobby Simpson.

He played first for the Ashfield Junior Technical School and while there was selected to represent the New South Wales Schoolboys. Then he played for one of the Sydney Central schools for a couple of seasons. He was 20 when he made his debut for New South Wales in 1945/6 and after scoring 68 against South Australia at Adelaide he scored a century against the Australian Services in only his third first-class match.

During the following season, Keith Miller signed to play for Rawtenstall in the Lancashire League, but felt obliged to change his mind under pressure from Don Bradman and the Australian cricket authorities. Rawtenstall's agent in Sydney tried several other players before turning to Ken Grieves, who eagerly signed and played in Miller's place for two years.

He joined Lancashire in 1949 and in only his second match, which was against Somerset at Old Trafford, he scored 68 and 91 and took eight wickets with his leg-breaks. His first century came at Oxford University in his fourth match and by early July the likeable Aussie had scored almost 900 runs and taken 57 wickets and had every chance of becoming the first Lancashire player for 14 years to complete the double. Unfortunately he had a difference of opinion with Lancashire captain Nigel Howard and bowled very little after that, taking only six more wickets before the end of the season. Grieves went on to score 1,047 runs and became the fourth player after Buddy Oldfield, Phil King and Ken Cranston to score 1,000 runs in his first season. He also held 32 catches but it was a great pity that his bowling talent was allowed to slip over the years.

During the winter of 1950 Grieves went on the Commonwealth tour of India and Ceylon. He scored heavily, making centuries in both matches against the Governor's XI.

Grieves' potential was quickly realised in the summer of 1950 when he held Lancashire's middle-order batting together as the county finished joint Champions with Surrey. He took 57 wickets to take his tally to 120 in his first two seasons. Surprisingly this constituted over half his eventual total in a 15-year career. Ken Grieves was also a world-class slip fielder and in 1950 established a new Lancashire record for the most outfield catches by taking 63. In 1951

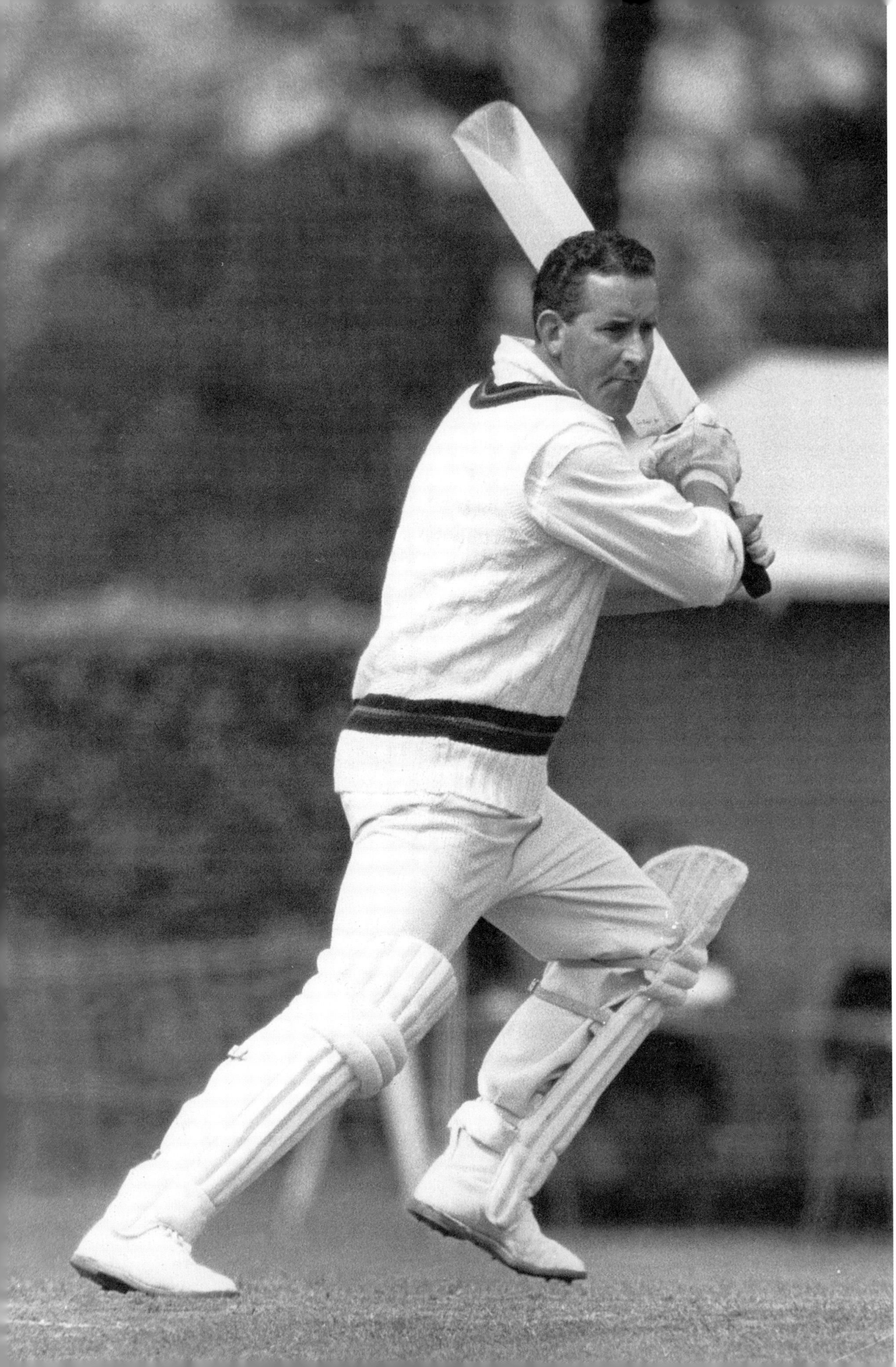

(LEP)

he equalled Dick Tyldesley's six catches in an innings and during the match against Sussex at Old Trafford he took his total to eight, which is the highest number of outfield catches by a player in a Lancashire match.

This dexterity with his hands was put to good use in the winter months, for Ken Grieves also played football as a goalkeeper. The appeal to come to England in 1947 was enhanced by the chance to play soccer professionally. After a trial with Manchester United, he joined Bury and played for them against Liverpool in a Lancashire Cup tie before starting his cricket duties. He later played for Bolton Wanderers and Stockport County.

In his first ten seasons with Lancashire Grieves passed 1,000 runs on eight occasions, including a career-best 224 against Cambridge University in 1957, and in 1959 2,253 runs came from his blade. When the Lancashire Committee turned to ex-Chorley captain Joe Blackledge to lead the team for the 1962 season, Ken Grieves must have felt more disappointed than anyone else. In fact, there were a large number of members who thought Grieves should have had the honour of captaining Lancashire on Cyril Washbrook's retirement in 1959, allowing Bob Barber time to come to terms with county cricket before he was burdened with the captaincy.

In 1962 Ken Grieves decided to give up county cricket and returned to the Leagues, this time as Stockport's professional in the Central Lancashire League. However, after the county finished second from bottom in 1962, the Lancashire Committee turned to Grieves for the 1963 season. This was the first season of one-day cricket, which seemed ideal for a player of Grieves' capabilities but ultimately poor team performances were to bring his downfall.

The county only improved marginally in the 1963 season though they did reach the semi-final of the new Gillette Cup competition, only to lose to Worcestershire. In 1964 despite the acquisition of West Indies Test bowler Sonny Ramadhin, the side struggled in fourteenth position and made another semi-final exit in the Gillette Cup. It was also Lancashire's centenary season and during the celebration match against the MCC, news was leaked that Grieves was one of four Lancashire players to be released for 1965.

One of Lancashire's finest players, he took part in 452 matches for the county – a figure surpassed by only seven other players. He scored 20,802 runs at 33.39, including 26 centuries, and took 235 wickets at 28.80 runs apiece. But he is best remembered for his brilliant fielding, particularly close to the wicket alongside Geoff Edrich and Jack Ikin and holds the county record for most catches in a career – 555, more than 200 ahead of second-highest, Archie MacLaren. Grieves' dismissal, despite allegations from other counties about the Lancashire players' bad language and ill discipline, was badly handled by the committee and without doubt reflected badly on the service given to Lancashire by the popular Grieves.

Eventually the bad feeling generated by his dismissal was forgotten and in 1978, Ken Grieves became a valued member of the Lancashire Committee. With his knowledge of the game and his advice to future players, he did much to help the county restore some of its former glory. After 13 years he stood down and was elected a life vice-president before his sudden death aged 66 at his Rawtenstall home in January 1992.

Frank Hayes

Born: 6 December 1946, Preston
County debut: Lancashire v Middlesex at Old Trafford, 1970

- He scored 22 centuries for Lancashire with a highest of 187 v India at Old Trafford in 1974.
- He scored 1,000 runs in a season for Lancashire on five occasions with a best of 1,283 at 37.73 in 1974.
- He appeared for England in nine Tests, scoring 106 not out against the West Indies at The Oval on his Test debut in 1973.
- He captained Lancashire from 1978 to 1980.
- He scored 34 (6, 4, 6, 6, 6, 6) off an over from Glamorgan's Malcolm Nash at Swansea in 1977 – then the second-highest total from a six-ball over without no-balls.

LANCASHIRE RECORD	
BATTING	
M	228
I	339
NO	48
Runs	10,899
HSc	187
Av	37.45
100	22
50	52
BOWLING	
Runs	11
Wkts	0

FRANK HAYES was born in Preston but his family moved to Marple in Cheshire when he was five. It was with the Marple club that this young batting prodigy made his first headlines, scoring centuries for the first team at the age of 14. The team dominated the Lancashire and Cheshire League.

Frank's father died in 1963 but he had already seen the impact that young Hayes was likely to make in the game of cricket. However, he had expressed a wish that his son continue with his studies, so even though Frank could have joined the Old Trafford staff at 18, he opted to go to Sheffield University where he gained second-class honours in physics and mathematics.

Hayes joined Lancashire in 1970 and everyone who saw him bat was convinced that he was potentially a great player. Everyone, that is, except Frank himself. Large scores in the 2nd XI, including an unbeaten 202 against Warwickshire, meant an early call-up to the first team.

In his first richly promising innings in the Championship he made 94 against Middlesex and tried to reach three figures with a glorious drive over the top, only to hole out at mid-on. When he followed this with 99 in the next match against Hampshire – this time he was stumped after a rash foray down the wicket – it must have seemed only a matter of time before the Championship hundred came along.

But the consistency of those first few innings was not maintained. He slipped out of Lancashire's powerful XI, with its run-hungry array – Wood, Pilling, the Lloyds, Engineer and the rest. Hayes batted at No.5 when the hunt for bonus points was quickening. This was neither the time nor place for a young cricketer trying to establish himself. After losing his place to Ken Snellgrove, Hayes fought his way back into the Lancashire side and did well without being spectacular. He was in the Lancashire side for the 1972 Gillette Cup final at Lord's, where he played well, and then with Derrick Robins' team in South Africa he again impressed sound judges with his obvious class, tested this time against some of the best players in the world.

(LEP)

After making a hundred in his first match for Lancashire in the 1973 season in the Benson & Hedges Cup, he made his long-awaited first-class century – 100 not out against Sussex at Hove. He followed it three days later with an unbeaten 154 off Glamorgan at Swansea (50 in 38 minutes, 100 in 90 minutes). This was followed by selection in the England XI for the third New Zealand Test, although he didn't play, and yet a further century against Nottinghamshire, his third for Lancashire in successive matches. Two half-centuries in the Test trial brought Hayes elevation into the Test arena against the West Indies at The Oval. The golden boy of English cricket hit a brilliant unbeaten 106 in the second innings to become the first Lancashire player to score a century on his Test debut. This performance ensured his place on the 1973/4 winter tour to the West Indies. In fact Frank Hayes played all his nine Tests against the West Indies, scoring 244 runs at an average of 15.25.

He made the highest score of his career, 187, against the 1974 Indian tourists at Old Trafford and this was one of his three centuries for the county that summer. The following season he hit the first of his three Roses centuries with a brilliant 101 at Headingley. In 1977 Hayes made an unbeaten 157 against Nottinghamshire at Trent Bridge, his highest Championship score of the season and his fifth century on the trot against Nottinghamshire. At the St Helen's Ground, Swansea, he hit Glamorgan's Malcolm Nash for 34 in one over with five sixes and one four, so nearly emulating Gary Sobers' record of six sixes in an over, which, of course, was off the same bowler.

After David Lloyd resigned the captaincy, Frank Hayes was chosen as the man to lead Lancashire in the 1978 season. Though the county moved from its position of sixteenth in 1977 to twelfth spot, Hayes was suffering from the effects of the break up of the successful side of the early 1970s. Lever, Shuttleworth and Engineer had left the county and Peter Lee suffered injury in the early matches of the season, leaving the county's pace attack almost decimated. However, Hayes' side did reach the semi-final of the Gillette Cup only to be beaten convincingly in the match against Sussex at Hove. In 1979 the county dropped one position to finish thirteenth in the Championship, but the following year finished fifteenth and still made little impact in the one-day competitions.

Frank Hayes hit 102 not out against the 1980 Australian tourists and passed 1,000 runs for the fifth time, scoring 622 runs in his last eight matches for an average of 62.20. That season Clive Lloyd was absent, touring with the West Indies, but it was announced that he would replace Hayes for the 1981 season.

Due to various injuries Frank Hayes played very little over the next four years and retired on medical advice after playing in the opening match of the 1984 season at Oxford University. However, in his testimonial season of 1983, which realised £40,768, he scored three centuries, his last an unbeaten 127 against Derbyshire at Blackpool.

Ken Higgs

Born: 14 January 1937, Kidsgrove, Staffordshire
County debut: Lancashire v Cambridge University at Fenner's, 1958

- He performed the hat-trick on two occasions for Lancashire – v Essex at Blackpool in 1960 and v Yorkshire at Headingley in 1968.
- He took 100 wickets in a season on five occasions with a best of 123 at 20.2 in 1960.
- He appeared in 15 Tests for England with a best return of 6 for 91 v the West Indies at Lord's in 1966.
- He shared the record England v West Indies tenth-wicket stand of 128 in 140 minutes with John Snow at The Oval in 1966, both batsmen scoring their maiden first-class fifties. This remains the highest tenth-wicket stand for England at home.
- He is the only bowler to take a hat-trick in a Lord's final (for Leicestershire v Surrey in the 1974 Benson & Hedges Cup).
- He shared in a record Leicestershire tenth-wicket stand of 228 with Ray Illingworth v Northamptonshire in 1977.

LANCASHIRE RECORD

BATTING

M	306
I	374
NO	131
Runs	2,655
HSc	60
Av	10.92
100	–
50	1

BOWLING

Runs	23,661
Wkts	1,033
Av	22.90
Best	7-19
5w	37
10w	5

BORN AMONG the pottery towns of Staffordshire, Ken Higgs came to the county game with an abundance of natural ability. He played soccer and cricket for the Secondary School in Tunstall but he lived only a few yards from the ground where the Meakins Pottery Works team played and it was here that his real development began. One evening he was asked to make up the number for the 2nd XI and although not then 12 years old, he was top scorer. His ability with the bat brought him many games with the Meakins team. At 15 he joined the ground staff of Port Vale, playing for the Colts, later as a centre-half in the reserves and on one occasion for the League side.

National Service saw him playing cricket for the Army with Harold Rhodes and following his release he returned to Port Vale and to Staffordshire League cricket where his consistent performances gained recognition in the Minor Counties side. By now several counties, including Leicestershire, Gloucestershire and Northamptonshire, had approached him, but it was on the suggestion of his Staffordshire captain, Denis Haynes, that he ultimately accepted Lancashire's offer.

His Championship debut in 1958 was startling, for against Hampshire he took 7 for 36 in nine overs to give Lancashire an easy target. But success in the county game has to be earned and he worked hard for his 66 wickets in the season. There was an expensive tendency in his early days to send a loose ball down the leg-side but consistent work in the nets under the watchful eye of coach Stan Worthington and a willingness to learn from his classic partner Brian Statham gradually improved his line and his increased effectiveness showed in his returns.

Spearheading the opening attack, he came in over 15 yards with an action that carried the full power of shoulder and body to get a considerable pace off the pitch. On a placid wicket at Ebbw Vale he bowled 22 overs to dismiss four of Glamorgan's first line batsmen for 37 runs. This was typical of his bowling – always aggressive, keeping the batsmen playing and making the odd ball move a little, even on the truest pitch.

Years of consistently successful bowling brought Higgs his Test debut in 1965 against South Africa. He partnered his county colleague Brian Statham in the third Test at The Oval and

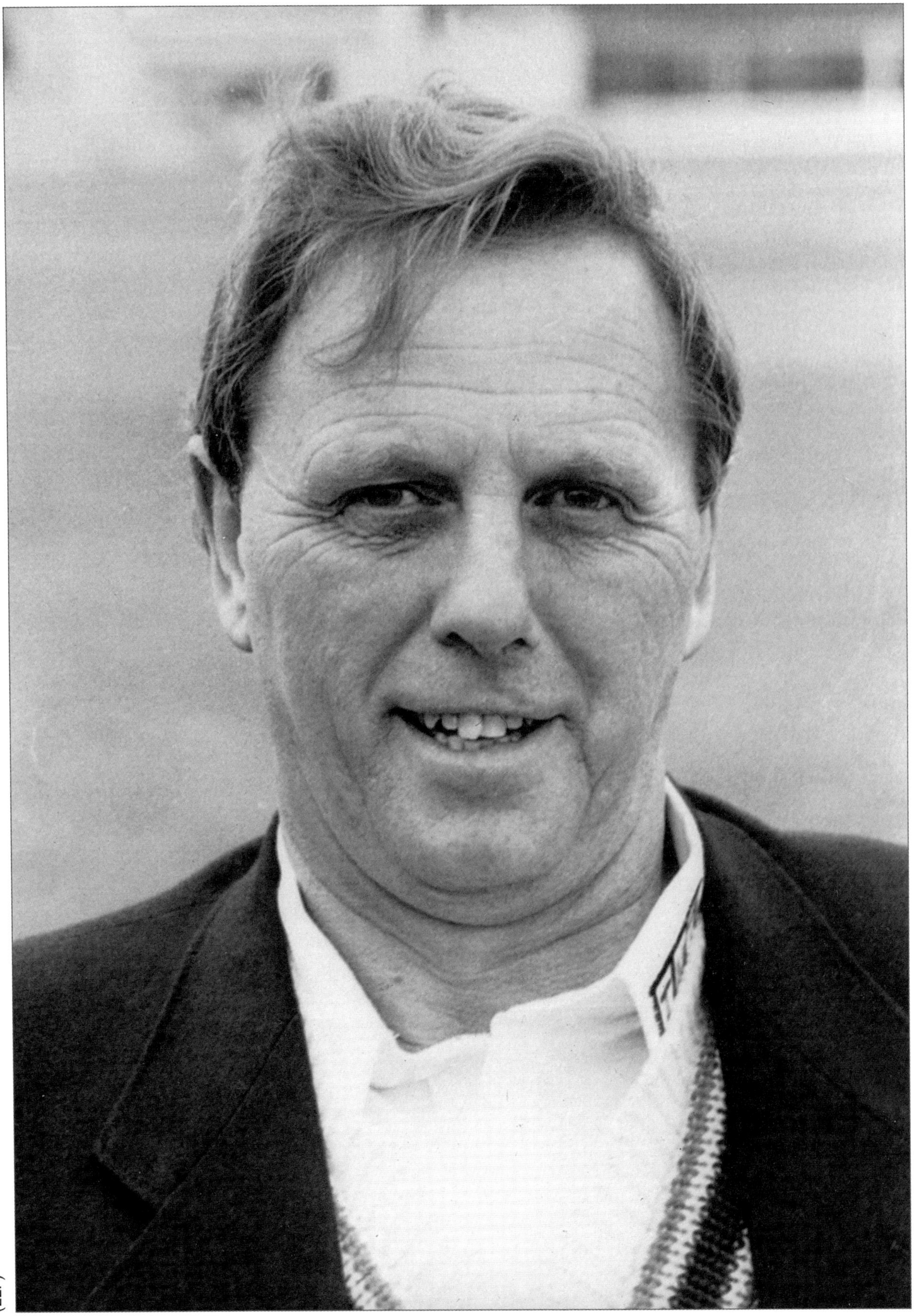

(LEP)

they shared 15 wickets in the match, with Higgs returning match figures of 8 for 143. He played 15 times for England against every major cricketing country, taking 71 wickets at an average of 20.74 runs apiece. He toured Australia and New Zealand in 1965/6 but illness and injuries confined him to one Test against Australia, although he recovered and played in all three in New Zealand. He also toured the West Indies in 1967/8 and was one of *Wisden*'s Five Cricketers of the Year in 1968.

After some disappointments and disagreements he left Lancashire at the end of the 1969 season and played for two years with Rishton in the Lancashire League. He owned a small hotel in Blackpool but found the tasks of washing the linen and cooking all the breakfasts before going to Old Trafford to play cricket rather too much, and so he gave it up.

Leicestershire persuaded him to return to the first-class game in 1972 and like so many other exiles who joined that team, he found a new lease of life and gave yeoman service to his adopted county.

His left-handed batting often proved stubborn as any, though occasionally a flashing off-drive was followed by his favourite sweep and lusty pull. He considered himself rather underrated and delighted in situations which allowed him to prove to himself that No.11 was not his true position. In fact, when he was out after a lengthy stay at the wicket he would take great pleasure in asking the earlier batsmen why they were in trouble! He did, after all, share a tenth-wicket partnership of 128 with John Snow against the West Indies at The Oval in 1966 – two runs short of the record for Test cricket. There was also the remarkable Leicestershire last-wicket stand against Northamptonshire at Grace Road in 1977. Going in at a total of 45 for 9, Higgs helped Illingworth (119 not out) to add 228 before running himself out for 98 – he tended to blame his more elderly partner for this mishap. This was his highest score in first-class cricket and the partnership was only eight runs short of the English county record for a last wicket.

He was originally a very good outfielder with a safe pair of hands but the passing years saw him develop into one of the best slip fielders in the game and he made catching look deceptively easy.

Ken Higgs always kept himself superbly fit. Believing in moderation in all things, he always had a long warm bath after each day's play instead of a shower. This was his recipe for keeping trim and supple, so essential for a pace bowler.

After playing in 165 first-class matches for Leicestershire, he retired in 1982 to become Leicestershire's coach. However, just to show how fit and how accurate a bowler he still was, he returned to the game in 1986 after a four-year-absence because of injuries. He took 5 for 22 against Yorkshire and he was then 49 years old.

His career figures were 1,536 wickets at a cost of 23.61 runs apiece. Ironically, his best analysis of 7 for 19 was achieved for Lancashire against Leicestershire in 1965 while his best for Leicestershire was 7 for 44 against Middlesex at Lord's in 1974. In his 12 seasons for Lancashire, Ken Higgs took 1,033 wickets at 22.90 runs each, a figure which had then been exceeded by only eight players.

Malcolm Hilton

Born: 2 August 1928, Chadderton, Oldham
Died: 8 July 1990
County debut: Lancashire v Sussex at Hove, 1946

- He bowled 68 balls before conceding a run for Lancashire v Sussex at Horsham in 1948.
- He took 103 wickets at an average of just 10.89 for Lancashire 2nd XI in 1949.
- He took 100 wickets in a season for Lancashire on four occasions with a best of 150 at 14.46 in 1956.
- He took eight wickets in an innings on two occasions with a best of 8 for 19 v New Zealand at Old Trafford in 1958.
- His best match figures were 14 for 88 v Somerset at Weston-super-Mare in 1956.
- His only century for Lancashire was 100 not out v Northamptonshire in 1955.
- He appeared in four Tests for England.

LANCASHIRE RECORD

BATTING

M	241
I	294
NO	35
Runs	3,140
HSc	100*
Av	12.12
100	1
50	5

BOWLING

Runs	17,419
Wkts	926
Av	18.81
Best	8–19
5w	48
10w	8

MALCOLM HILTON, the son of a painter and decorator, played his early cricket with Werneth in the Central Lancashire League and made his name as a left-arm spinner after being steered away from his ambition to be a fast bowler. He made his debut for Lancashire in the last match of 1946 when he was just 18 years old and was still only 33 when he played his last match in 1961. In the intervening years he took 926 wickets for Lancashire at an average of 18.81 and took 1,000 in all matches.

Hilton was still only 19 and in his third first-class game when he dismissed Don Bradman twice in Lancashire's match against the Australians at Old Trafford. Bradman had scored 765 runs in his first six innings of the Australian tour with a lowest score of 81, yet here he was bowled for 11 by the unknown Hilton in the first innings and stumped for 43 in the second after being beaten three times. Not surprisingly the young Hilton was thrust into the limelight and when Lancashire went to London for their next match against Middlesex at Lord's, a whole line of pressmen were waiting on the platform at Euston to talk to the Oldham-born spinner. Yet despite his success against Bradman, he was left out of the team to play at MCC's headquarters!

Malcolm Hilton did not become a regular in the Lancashire team until 1950 when he took 127 wickets at 15.32 for the county and made the first of his four Test appearances for England against the West Indies. His second Test came the following year against South Africa and in his two Tests in India in the winter of 1951/2 under the captaincy of Nigel Howard, who was also his captain at Lancashire, he took 11 wickets at only 17.35 runs apiece.

He never played for England again. During his short international career he took 15 wickets at 33.64 runs each, though his best season was still to come. In 1956 he took 150 wickets at under 15 runs apiece for Lancashire and was one of *Wisden*'s Cricketers of the Year. His best Championship bowling came that year with figures of 8 for 39 against Somerset at Weston-super-Mare and a match return of 14 for 88. This was the fourth and last time that Hilton took 100 wickets for Lancashire. He lost his regular place in the Lancashire side and took just 20 wickets in 1959 – the season in which he reached his 1,000 first-class wickets. Hilton did not play in 1960 and he retired in 1961 after playing in three matches.

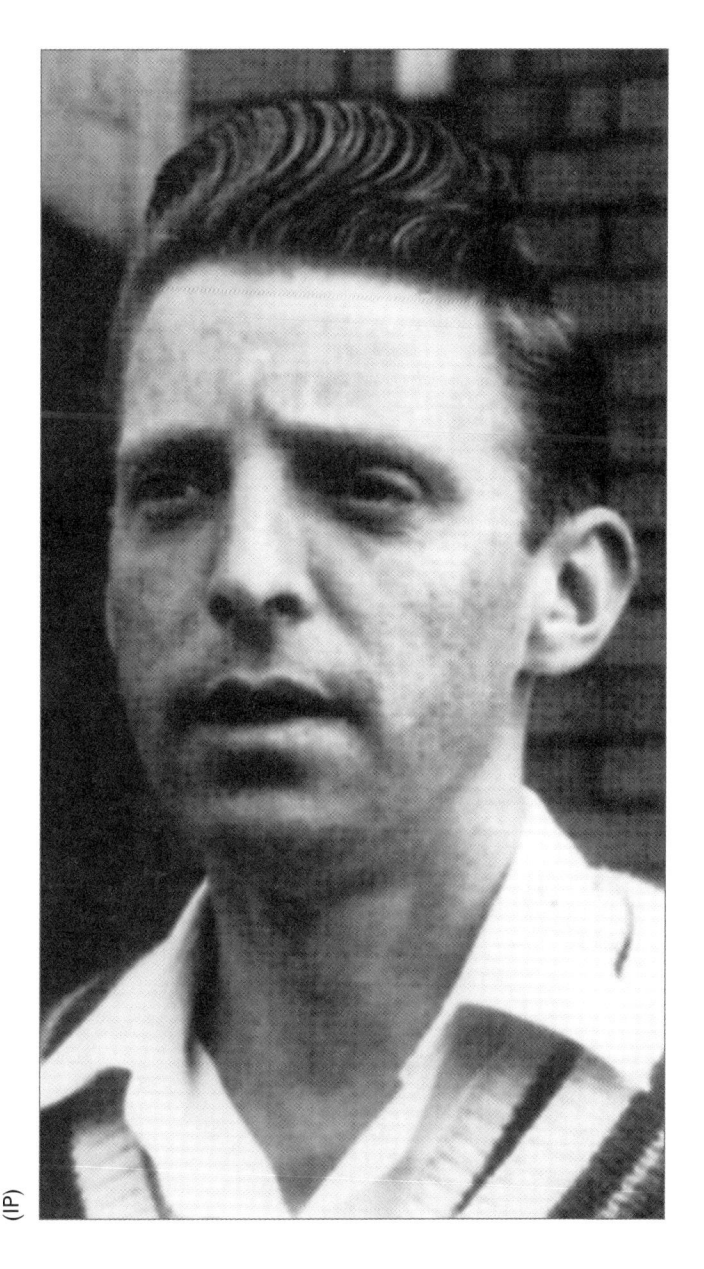

His only century came in 1955 when batting at No.9 for Lancashire in their match at Northampton. He reached his hundred in exactly two hours on a wicket which was so perfect that when he bowled he took only George Tribe's wicket and that for 137 runs in 61 overs.

He departed from the first-class scene at an age when many spinners are just reaching their peak. He had simply lost his control. But Hilton, who always looked on the funny side of life, never complained. When things were not going well, he would ask Cyril Washbrook, the Lancashire captain, for a deep square leg. More often than not, Hilton's request was turned down and he just got on with his bowling.

After leaving Old Trafford, he played as professional with Oldham and Radcliffe in the Lancashire League before returning to Werneth as captain. A great one for the Stanley Holloway monologues, he was ill for some time before dying at his home in Oldham in July 1990, still only 61.

Nigel Howard

Born: 18 May 1925, Gee Cross, Hyde
Died: 31 May 1979
County debut: Lancashire v Middlesex at Old Trafford, 1946

LANCASHIRE RECORD	
BATTING	
M	170
I	234
NO	29
Runs	5,526
HSc	145
Av	26.95
100	3
50	33
BOWLING	
Runs	23
Wkts	0

- He scored three centuries for Lancashire with a highest of 145 v Derbyshire at Old Trafford in 1948.
- He captained Lancashire from 1949 to 1953, leading the county to the joint-Champions status in 1950.
- He appeared in four Tests for England, captaining his country in all of them.

NIGEL HOWARD was a talented sportsman. He captained England in four Tests during the MCC tour of India and Pakistan in 1951/2 and he was the youngest-ever captain of Lancashire from 1949 to 1953 before retiring from the game to concentrate on the family textile business. He later became a Lancashire Committee member and was chairman of the cricket committee during the county's successful run in the one-day Gillette Cup and John Player Sunday League competitions. Elected as a vice-president of Lancashire County Cricket Club, he also played for Cheshire at hockey and golf, eventually becoming a member of the committee of the Royal and Ancient golf club.

Nigel was a regular at Old Trafford from a very young age. His father, Major Rupert Howard, who had played for Lancashire between the wars and had scored 88 not out on his debut, was secretary at Old Trafford from 1932 to 1948.

Educated at Rossall School (like Lancashire's first captain, Edmund Rowley) and later Manchester University, Nigel Howard made his debut for the county in 1946. His younger brother Barry, who played in 32 matches between 1947 and 1951, played in the same side as Nigel. Barry was to become president of Lancashire in 1987/8, giving the family positions as president, captain and secretary in the years following the Second World War.

Nigel Howard did not attain a regular place in the Lancashire line-up until 1948 when he made his maiden century – 145 against Derbyshire at Old Trafford. Another of his three centuries came against Kent at Maidstone in 1952 where he went in just before tea and was 138 not out at the close.

He was elected captain of Lancashire for the 1949 season at the age of 24, the youngest in the county's history. The side Howard inherited was moving towards blooding more youngsters with Bob Berry, Malcolm Hilton, Roy Tattersall and Alan Wharton all playing regularly. Yet despite Washbrook, Place, Pollard, Edrich and Ikin providing the experience, Howard's side ended the season in eleventh place in the Championship.

In 1950 his captaincy helped to bring the title of joint Champions to Lancashire. He scored an unbeaten 101 against Gloucestershire at Old Trafford and ended the season with 1,174 runs at an average of 37.97. In the last match against Surrey at The Oval Lancashire only needed four points from a first innings lead, assuming Surrey did not win the match to take the title outright, but despite a brave 51 from Howard, Lancashire could only muster 221. Surrey themselves had a chance of the title but after a fine 92 by Peter May, the match petered out into a boring draw with only 711 runs scored in 17 hours' play.

In 1951 Howard's form was recognised by the captaincy of the Gentlemen v Players – Tattersall, Statham, Ikin and Hilton represented the players. Freddie Brown had been chosen to captain the Gentlemen, but injury kept him away. Then the leadership was passed to Norman Yardley, but a few minutes before the match was due to begin he gave the honour to Howard so that he could gain experience of handling a representative side before taking the MCC team to India and Pakistan. The Players won by 21 runs with only three minutes left! Howard's contributions were 1 and 0 – he was stumped by Godfrey Evans off Tattersall in the second innings! At county level, Howard's side fell away towards the end of the 1951 season to finish third. He played in four Tests for England, all of them in India in 1951/2 when he captained a team which also included other Lancashire players Brian Statham, Roy Tattersall and Malcolm Hilton.

A fine batsman who liked to force the pace, he sometimes opened the batting when accepting the challenge of a declaration, but more usually he featured in the middle order. He had a very disappointing 1952 season, dropping himself at one stage because of his poor form. Despite this Lancashire still held on to third place in the Championship.

As a captain, Howard was concerned with the well-being of his team, and in particular was very involved with the development of such fine cricketers as Brian Statham, Roy Tattersall and Malcolm Hilton. His own personal success mattered very little to him, but the success of the team was of paramount importance.

Though Lancashire ended the 1953 season in third place in the Championship, Nigel Howard, at the age of 28, felt he could no longer continue to play full-time cricket and retired to concentrate on the family textile business. He died at the tragically young age of 54 in 1979 at his home on the Isle of Man, three years after moving there. He was the last captain to lead Lancashire to the County Championship.

David Hughes

Born: 13 May 1947, Newton-le-Willows
County debut: Lancashire v Oxford University at Old Trafford, 1967

- He hit Gloucestershire's John Mortimore for 24 in one over in the Gillette Cup semi-final of 1971.
- He went two better in the 1976 final of the Gillette Cup, hitting Northamptonshire's Indian Test spinner Bishen Bedi for 26 off the last over in Lancashire's innings.
- He scored eight centuries for Lancashire with a highest of 153 v Glamorgan at Old Trafford in 1983.
- He captained Lancashire from 1987 to 1991 and at the end of his first season in charge he was voted captain of the year. He led the county to success as winners of the Refuge Assurance Cup in 1988, the Refuge Assurance League in 1989 and both the Benson & Hedges Cup and NatWest Trophy in 1990.

LANCASHIRE RECORD	
BATTING	
M	436
I	567
NO	107
Runs	10,126
HSc	153
Av	22.01
100	8
50	45
BOWLING	
Runs	18,971
Wkts	637
Av	29.78
Best	7–24
5w	20
10w	2

DAVID HUGHES' reputation suffers from the over-simplification of collective memory: all that the casual cricket follower will remember about him is his remarkable match-winning innings in the Old Trafford murk against Gloucestershire in the Gillette Cup semi-final of 1971. Gloucestershire had batted first and reached 229 for 6. After the loss of an hour to the rain, it was clear that the game would end late or carry on to a second day. The irony was that John Mortimore, who had bowled his side to the brink of victory, was cast by fickle chance as the player who would finally bring about Gloucestershire's defeat. With overs still in the bank for Davey and Procter, Mortimore was called upon to bowl and Hughes, in the sure knowledge that it would be too dark at 8.45 pm to lay a bat upon the faster men, set about the decimation of poor Mortimore.

He struck the first ball of the fifty-sixth over to extra-cover for four, the second went for six to long-on, the third for two to extra-cover, the fourth to wide long-on for two, the fifth was cover driven for four and the sixth sailed high to long-on for another six. Now the scores were level and the way was open for Jack Bond to make the winning run. Hughes may have finished with just 26 not out but it was enough to transform him into a Lancastrian folk-hero overnight.

David was born at Newton-le-Willows. His father Lloyd was a professional in the Bolton League who was consistently skilful with his in-swing bowling and had one haul of ten wickets to his credit. David was a product of the Manchester Association and his home-town team of Newton-le-Willows before he joined Bolton League side Farnworth. He was signed by Lancashire in 1967 just prior to the one-day explosion in the game.

The Gillette Cup was retained in the summer of 1971 as Lancashire beat Kent by 24 runs in the final. While Hughes' batting had won the semi-final encounter with Gloucestershire, it was his left-arm spin bowling in tandem with the off-spin of Jack Simmons that was to play an important part in the Jack Bond era. During the 1970 and 1971 seasons Hughes bowled more than 800 overs and took 82 wickets in each season. In the five summers that Bond was captain he took 296 wickets but when Bond went, Hughes bowled less and seemed to lose it.

As his bowling declined, his batting came to the fore. In the 1976 Gillette Cup final Hughes went one better than his semi-final performance of two years earlier, hitting Indian spin bowler Bishen Bedi, then of Northamptonshire, for 26 off the last over of Lancashire's innings.

(LEP)

It was during this time that Hughes and Jack Simmons made their mark on the Tasmanian cricketing scene, both gaining high praise as they helped to develop the game in the Australian state.

In 1981 Hughes reached 1,000 runs for the first time in his career. He scored a masterly 87 against Somerset and Joel Garner's world-class fast-medium bowling in May and then followed it with an even more noteworthy achievement: it was a long time to wait for a maiden Championship century but David Hughes registered his at Old Trafford against Warwickshire in June, 14 years after he made his debut for the county. It was a superb innings and, in the face of fiery bowling from Bob Willis, helped to rescue Lancashire from yet another worrying situation.

The following summer was Hughes' best all-round season, when he bettered the previous season's batting performance, scoring 1,303 runs at an average of 48.25, and headed the Lancashire bowling averages with 31 wickets at 25.45 runs apiece. Although 1983 was not as successful, Hughes hit his highest-ever score of 153 against Glamorgan at Old Trafford. A testimonial that summer of £76,000 showed the high value Lancashire placed on Hughes. However, after 1983 he was unable to maintain this performance and increasingly slipped into the second team.

By 1986 Hughes was captaining the 2nd XI in partnership with Alan Ormrod, so successfully that they led the team to the Championship. Within weeks, Hughes found himself propelled to the captaincy of the first team, with Ormrod appointed coach. In his first season in charge he came desperately close to leading Lancashire to their first outright Championship since 1934 and was chosen as one of *Wisden*'s Five Cricketers of the Year. He was also voted Captain of the Year by the Cricket Writers' Club. As a captain, Hughes led the side from the front, was always positive and always attacking and in 1988 Lancashire beat Worcestershire in the first ever Refuge Assurance Cup final. In 1989 Hughes' side finished fourth in the Championship but won the Sunday League Trophy for the first time since 1970. The following season Lancashire took both the NatWest Trophy and the Benson & Hedges Cup: they were now one of the game's finest sides.

In 1991 Hughes decided to leave himself out of the Benson & Hedges Cup final at Lord's when Worcestershire avenged their defeat of the previous season and didn't play again for the county. One of the best all-rounders to captain Lancashire, he lifted the county's fortunes and standing.

Jack Ikin

Born: 7 March 1918, Bignall End, Staffordshire
Died: 15 September 1984
County debut: Lancashire v West Indies at Old Trafford, 1939

- In the match against Nottinghamshire at Old Trafford in 1947 he scored 67 and 85 not out and had match figures of 11 for 119.
- He carried his bat through an innings on two occasions with a best of 125 not out v Surrey at The Oval in 1951.
- He scored 1,000 runs in a season on ten occasions with a best of 1,729 at 36.78 in 1955.
- He performed the hat-trick v Somerset at Taunton in 1949.
- He scored 23 centuries for Lancashire with a highest of 192 v Oxford University at The Parks in 1951.
- He appeared in 18 Tests for England.
- He held five catches in an innings for MCC v Auckland in 1946/7 to equal the New Zealand record.

LANCASHIRE RECORD

BATTING

M	288
I	431
NO	51
Runs	14,327
HSc	192
Av	37.70
100	23
50	86

BOWLING

Runs	8,005
Wkts	278
Av	28.79
Best	6–21
5w	10
10w	1

BORN AT Bignall End, Jack Ikin began his career with his home-town club in the North Staffordshire League. He was only 16 when he first played for Staffordshire in the Minor Counties Championship and among his team-mates was Sydney Barnes, then aged 61. In 1928, when he headed the batting, he was picked for the Minor Counties against Oxford University.

He made his first appearance for Lancashire in 1939 and took his first wicket in first-class cricket – that of the great George Headley – before going into the Army where he served as a 'Desert Rat'. When the war was over Ikin established himself in the Lancashire team. In 1946 he scored 1,296 runs, took five wickets and held 55 catches, and was actually selected for England in the first post-war Test match against India before he was capped by Lancashire. He had only played in 18 first-class matches though he was regarded as the ideal team man, his war service reflecting his courage, lack of selfishness and enthusiasm.

He was a member of the MCC team who went to Australia and New Zealand in 1946/7. At Sydney his 60 made in three hours was the second-highest innings in a total of 255, while at Melbourne in a desperate situation he made 48 and helped Yardley to score 113 in two hours. In the fifth Test, again at Sydney, he made a pair but held three good catches. During 1947/8 he was a member of Gubby Allen's side to the West Indies, but failed to perform and his only other tour was with a Commonwealth team to India in 1950/1. Here he had the most prolific season of his career, heading the averages in the unofficial Tests with 625 runs at an average of 89.28. An injury forced him to refuse the MCC tour to India the following winter.

In 1951 he withstood South Africa's Cuan McCarthy unflinchingly in three Tests, making 51 at Lord's and sharing in an opening stand of 121 with Len Hutton at Old Trafford. In 1952 he made 53 against India at The Oval and in 1955, after a three-year absence from the international scene, he was recalled as one of five left-handers to counter Goddard's leg theory, but the experiment was not a success and Ikin, opening the batting with Brian Close, scored 17 and 0 in what was to be his last Test.

Ikin had played in 18 Tests for England between 1946 and 1955, scoring 606 runs at 20.89, taking three wickets and holding 31 catches. These figures naturally beg the question,

(LEP)

why was he picked so often and for so long? The answer is that though at the time England had such batsmen as Hutton, Washbrook, Compton and Edrich and at the end of the period May and Cowdrey, the depth of batting seen before the war was lacking; two or three reliable players – and Ikin was certainly one of these – were needed to support the stars and crises were frequent. He was essentially a sound and determined player who could be trusted not to throw his wicket away. He was adaptable and equally happy to open or go in at six or seven. Above all, he was a superb fielder, whether at short leg or in the slips. Though he never made a big score for England, he often played bravely when runs were wanted.

Ikin scored 23 centuries for Lancashire with a highest of 192 against Oxford University at The Parks in 1951 and when he hit 167 for the county against New Zealand at Old Trafford in 1949, he added 248 with Ken Grieves for the fourth wicket. In 1948 he came close to adding two more hundreds to his total. A century was nearly his in Lancashire's match against the Australians at Old Trafford when Don Bradman, the Australian captain, forced the follow-on. Bradman then scored a fine 133 on what was his last appearance at the ground. Lancashire comfortably played out time, although with just minutes to go before the end of the match Bradman took the new ball. Ray Lindwall bowled Ikin for 99. It was the second time in successive games that Ikin had been dismissed one short of his hundred, having been out for 99 in the previous game against Essex at Blackpool.

His best piece of bowling was 6 for 21 (11 for 119 in the match) against Nottinghamshire at Old Trafford in 1947 and two years later he achieved the hat-trick against Somerset at Taunton.

Ikin's career with Lancashire extended to 1957 and consisted of 288 matches in which he scored 14,327 runs and took 278 wickets. However, his career was far from over when he left the county. He rejoined Staffordshire and continued to play for them until 1968, scoring heavily and captaining the side from 1957 to 1967.

Jack Ikin was assistant-manager to S.C. Griffith on the MCC tour of Australia and New Zealand in 1965/6 and in 1972 he managed the first England Young Cricketers' side to the West Indies. For many years he was coach at Denstone School, where he was a much loved and respected figure. He was elected an Honorary Cricketing Member of MCC.

Peter Lever

Born: 17 September 1940, Todmorden
County debut: Lancashire v Cambridge University at Old Trafford, 1960

- He performed the hat-trick v Nottinghamshire at Old Trafford in 1969.
- His best bowling for Lancashire was 7 for 70 v Glamorgan at Old Trafford in 1972.
- He appeared in 17 Tests for England with a best performance of 6 for 38 v Australia at Melbourne in 1974/5 – this included a spell of 4 wickets for 5 runs.
- His 88 not out v India at Old Trafford in 1971 was his highest first-class score and he made it in a record England v India eighth-wicket stand of 168 with Ray Illingworth.
- He took 7 for 83 against the Rest of the World side on his unofficial England debut in 1970.

LANCASHIRE RECORD

BATTING

M	268
I	285
NO	59
Runs	3,073
HSc	83
Av	13.59
100	–
50	9

BOWLING

Runs	17,647
Wkts	716
Av	24.64
Best	7–70
5w	25
10w	2

PETER LEVER was nearly 30 when he played for England against the Rest of the World side in 1970. Replacing Tony Greig in the last game of the series and coming on as second change after Snow, Old and Wilson, he produced what were then the best figures of his career – 7 for 83 – in the first innings of the World XI. They were the worthwhile wickets of Barlow, Graeme Pollock, Mushtaq, Sobers, Clive Lloyd, Procter and Intikhab. The Saturday crowd had turned up to watch Pollock and Sobers continue their spectacular partnership of the previous day, but instead they saw Peter Lever tying them down, putting them out and bowling himself into the side for Australia.

Hardly any cricketer, least of all a pace bowler who has never taken a hundred wickets in a season, can hope to be chosen for England for the first time within a month of his thirtieth birthday but when that happened to Peter Lever, he accepted the opportunity with the excitement and gratitude of a modest man.

Omitted for the first Test in Australia, he bowled his way in for the second; proved an admirable foil to John Snow in the decisive breakthrough in the fourth; was the most effective England bowler in the sixth; and with three good and economical wickets in the first innings and Greg Chappell in the second, played an important part in the winning of the seventh, which gave England the Ashes. It was obvious that he was a good tourist.

Left out of the first Indian Test in the summer of 1971, he came back in the second at Old Trafford when his 5 for 70 and an innings of 88 not out gave England a winning chance that was destroyed by rain. He also took part in two valuable batting partnerships, both wicket records for those Test series: 149 in 133 minutes with Alan Knott for the seventh wicket against New Zealand and 168 with Ray Illingworth for the eighth in the 1971 Indian Test at Lord's.

Born in the 'border town' of Todmorden – since the 1890s legally in Yorkshire but spiritually in Lancashire by virtue of being a cotton rather than a woollen town – he was the son of a textile engineer. His parents pushed him into cricket by taking him along to net practice at the Todmorden Cricket Club. He came under the influence of Neil Dansie, the South Australian state player who had a spell as professional with Todmorden in the 1950s. Having a brother like Colin Lever also helped, for in 1960 he went along to Old Trafford for a trial and was offered a seasonal contract from April to September but because of Todmorden's geographical location, he could not play for the first or second XI until he had been specially registered.

(LEP)

He first appeared for Lancashire in the summer of 1960 when he was 19 but he also studied hard for a three-year course at Leeds City and Carnegie Physical Education College. He served long and earnestly in the shadow of England bowlers Brian Statham and Ken Higgs and was not capped until 1965. Even in that season he played in only 14 of the county's 28 Championship matches. Subsequently the more explosive Ken Shuttleworth appeared superficially a better prospect and was chosen in the first of the England v Rest of the World matches.

In 1963 and 1966 in particular Peter Lever batted well enough to hold a middle-order place in the Lancashire line-up in addition to providing support for Statham and Higgs. In both of these seasons he scored over 500 runs and took more than 50 wickets, but once he began to play for England, his batting declined.

Peter Lever always gave 100 per cent; occasionally it was argued that his run-up was too long but it was the approach of one set upon lifting the natural medium-pace to the highest level consonant with control. His stamina – doggedly developed by regular cross-country running – and application meant that he could bowl long spells without loss of control or enthusiasm. The spark which lifted him above some others was his ability to make the ball – new or worn – that pitched on the right-hander's stumps leave the bat late and with all the life the pitch would allow. These merits made Lever an honest and respected performer at the highest level of cricket.

After an absence of two years he was recalled to England's Test team for the 1974/5 Australasian tour. In Australia he took 0 for 111 in the first Test, missed the middle four and astounded the opposition with 6 for 38 on the first morning at Melbourne, placing Australia in a hopeless position. Then at Auckland during the first New Zealand Test match his name appeared on all the front pages when a short ball he bowled to Ewan Chatfield, New Zealand's No.11, knocked Chatfield unconscious. Chatfield's life was saved by immediate medical attention. Lever played only once against the 1975 Australians, taking his total of wickets in his 17 Tests to 41 at an average of 36.80 runs apiece.

Peter Lever was also a vital member of Lancashire's team of the early 1970s and in 167 limited-overs appearances he had the outstanding return of 256 wickets at 17.53 runs each. By the time the popular bowler retired shortly before the start of the 1977 season, he had played in 268 first-class matches for Lancashire and had taken 716 wickets at 24.64 runs apiece.

Clive Lloyd

Born: 31 August 1944, Queenstown, Georgetown, British Guyana
County debut: Lancashire v Australia at Old Trafford, 1968

- He scored 30 centuries for Lancashire with a highest total of 217 not out v Warwickshire at Old Trafford in 1971.
- He scored 1,000 runs in a season on seven occasions with a best of 1,458 at 63.39 in 1974.
- He captained Lancashire from 1981 to 1983 and again in 1986.
- He appeared in 110 Tests for the West Indies (74 as captain – a record) scoring 7,515 runs at 46.67. His highest Test score is 242 not out v India at Bombay in 1974/5.
- He scored 200 not out for the West Indies v Glamorgan at Swansea in 1976 to equal the record for the fastest-ever double century in first-class cricket.

LANCASHIRE RECORD

BATTING

M	219
I	326
NO	42
Runs	12,764
HSc	217*
Av	44.94
100	30
50	71

BOWLING

Runs	1,809
Wkts	55
Av	32.89
Best	4-48
5w	–
10w	–

NO PLAYER has made as much of an impact on Lancashire cricket as Clive Hubert Lloyd. Arguably Lancashire's greatest-ever batsman, he was born in Georgetown, Guyana, on 31 August 1944. He was educated in his native town and at the age of 12, while trying to separate two fighting school friends, he received a blow in the eye. His eyesight was affected and he has been obliged to wear spectacles ever since. Like many another West Indian lad he was attracted to cricket early and learned the game by playing with older boys, among them his cousin Lance Gibbs, who was later to take 312 Test wickets for the West Indies. Clive made his Guyana debut in 1963/4 against Jamaica, following it up with a Test debut for the West Indies in 1966/7 against India.

In 1967 he came to England to play as a professional for Haslingden in the Lancashire League. It wasn't only the League bowlers who suffered the summary consequence of the blows from the immense bat. Haslingden members will recall with many a chuckle how Lloyd once felled his batting partner who turned his back and took the full force of a straight drive on his rump! It was in League cricket that Lloyd abandoned his leg-breaks for the more utilitarian medium-pace which he was subsequently to bowl in Test and county cricket.

Lloyd accepted a contract with Lancashire when his Haslingden engagement expired. He played in one match in 1968 against the touring Australians before linking up with the county in 1969. It was then that his namesake, David, pointed out to everybody that there were now two Lloyds in the Lancashire side and both were left-handed, but no one need worry because it was easy to tell them apart – one wore glasses!

Though he failed to score a century in 1969, Lloyd helped Lancashire win the new John Player League. It was certainly no coincidence that Lloyd's arrival in the Lancashire side was followed by the emergence of the extra dimension of class that enabled the county to dominate the English game at one-day level.

Lloyd's first century for Lancashire came the following season in the match against Kent at Dartford. The innings of 163 lasted only 145 minutes and included seven sixes. Lloyd brought much joy to Lancashire cricket that year with 44 sixes, 25 of them in first-class matches. He hit another century at Oxford and his first at Old Trafford was 102 against Gloucestershire. In the John Player League he scored 134 not out against Somerset – Lancashire's highest score in the competition until it was beaten by Andy Flintoff in 1999. To make the 1970 season

(MEN)

complete, he played for the Rest of the World in the series against England and got centuries at Trent Bridge and Edgbaston.

Until 1991 Lloyd also held the county's highest score in the Benson & Hedges Cup competition with 124 not out against Warwickshire. In fact, Warwickshire were a team that Clive Lloyd seemed to take a particular liking to: his highest score for Lancashire of 217 not out came against Warwickshire at Old Trafford in 1971 and the Edgbaston side were Lancashire's opponents in the 1972 Gillette Cup final when Lloyd scored a brilliant match-winning 126.

The captaincy of the West Indies was handed to him in 1974 and he was to hold the position for eleven seasons. West Indies had long been associated with producing world-class players, but they had struggled to find any consistency as a team. Leading from the front, Clive Lloyd changed all that and made them into one of the most successful and feared international sides. During his first series as captain he hit a Test century in 102 minutes against India at Bangalore. He went on to 163 with two sixes and 22 fours, an innings that is still the fastest century on record in West Indies Test matches. In the same series he achieved the highest score of his Test career – 242 not out in a West Indies total of 604 at Bombay.

But it was 1975 that provided something special: a World Cup year, a brilliant summer in England and six centuries for Lancashire, four of them in successive matches. Four of his hundreds were reached in 130 minutes or under and the slowest, against Hampshire at Liverpool, was barely over two-and-a-half hours. Lloyd's fastest century in 1975 came in 118 minutes against Nottinghamshire at Trent Bridge, but his most spectacular came in a freak of a game against Derbyshire at Buxton, his last before joining the West Indies for the World Cup. He scored 147 not out in 167 minutes, the last 47 runs coming in 37 minutes as he finished with eight sixes and 15 fours before Lancashire's innings closed at 477 for 5 on a lovely sunny Saturday. It snowed the following Monday, 2 June! On the Tuesday Derbyshire were bowled out for 42 and 87 to lose by an innings and 348 runs to Lancashire – an innings and 38 runs to Clive Lloyd.

He led West Indies to victory in the 1975 Prudential World Cup, scoring 102 off 82 balls against Australia in the final. Lloyd then returned to Old Trafford in August and hit 751 runs (average 107.28) that month including four centuries. He scored two centuries in the John Player League in 98 and 80 minutes and that winter went to Australia where a century against Western Australia took just 78 minutes.

Lloyd was having trouble with his knees around this time and operations were inevitable. They were performed in 1977, soon after one of his most stunning innings. By this time both knees were causing problems and he shifted the weight from one to the other while hitting sixes in a Gillette Cup match against Surrey at Old Trafford; his total was 86 but Lancashire still lost by four wickets. At the end of 1980, when Gillette ended their sponsorship, Clive Lloyd was awarded the man-of-the-series trophy as the player who had made the highest contribution.

When Jack Bond returned to the county as team manager in 1981, Lloyd was elected captain of Lancashire to replace Frank Hayes. Unfortunately during his three-year spell in charge (and in a further year as captain in 1986), Clive could not produce the winning formula he had at international level. The only consolation in 1981 was Lancashire's success in the seven-a-side competition sponsored by Lambert & Butler in which Lloyd dominated all of the four matches Lancashire played. During 1982 Lloyd hit his sixth century against Yorkshire, the most by a Lancashire player in a Roses match to date. In 1983 he only appeared in 11 Championship matches due to his captaining the West Indies in the Prudential World Cup, where they were beaten finalists.

Lloyd was away all of the 1984 season captaining the West Indies touring team and when he returned the following summer, the county faced the problem of choosing just one overseas player from a possible three. Pat Patterson won the vote on most occasions.

Surprisingly Lloyd was named captain for 1986 but because Patterson was needed to spearhead the Lancashire attack, Lloyd only played in seven of the 24 Championship matches. However, he topped the one-day averages and led the county to the NatWest final at Lord's. On an emotional day he was given a standing ovation to and from the wicket; sadly he was dismissed without scoring. His career was at an end.

In first-class matches for Lancashire he scored 12,764 runs and averaged 44.94, the second highest average (behind Ernest Tyldesley) by a Lancashire player. At international level he appeared in 110 Tests and scored 7,515 runs for an average of 46.67. He was without doubt one of the world's finest batsmen.

David Lloyd

Born: 18 March 1947, Accrington
County debut: Lancashire v Middlesex at Old Trafford, 1965

- He scored 1,000 runs in a season on ten occasions with a best of 1,510 at 47.18 in 1972.
- With Mike Denness he shared in century stands in both innings of the match between MCC and Warwickshire at Lord's in 1973 (138 and 181).
- He scored 37 centuries for Lancashire with a highest of 195 v Gloucestershire at Old Trafford in 1973.
- In 1979 he scored hundreds – 116 and 104 not out – in each innings of the match against Worcestershire at Southport.
- He captained Lancashire from 1973 to 1977, leading the county to the Gillette Cup in 1975.
- He appeared in nine Tests for England. His 214 v India at Edgbaston in 1974 was made in 448 minutes off 396 balls and remained the highest score of his first-class career. He was on the field throughout the match.

LANCASHIRE RECORD

BATTING

M	378
I	605
NO	70
Runs	17,877
HSc	195
Av	33.41
100	37
50	86

BOWLING

Runs	7,007
Wkts	234
Av	29.94
Best	7–38
5w	5
10w	1

BROUGHT UP in the Lancashire League at his home-town club, Accrington, David Lloyd played his first game at the age of 15 and was pitch-forked into opposition against some of the world's leading players. The fact that he survived against the likes of Wes Hall, Bobby Simpson and Eddie Barlow is a tribute to his resilience.

There was a time when David Lloyd was a real worrier and his initiation into the first-class game in 1965 cannot have been exactly reassuring because he notched a pair against Middlesex, bowled by Titmus in the first innings and caught behind off Bick in the second; still, after a start like that only improvement could follow and of course it did. He finished the season with 17 Championship wickets at 32 runs apiece and a humble batting average of 12, but he had been top-scorer with 44 in the second innings of Lancashire's match with Northamptonshire at Old Trafford.

When he first turned up at Old Trafford, Lloyd was registered as a highly promising slow left-hand bowler with batting possibilities. Like many young players he reacted to what he interpreted as a vote of confidence after an inauspicious start and a period of hard, grafting apprenticeship ending in 1968 with the award of his county cap. With Jack Bond's appointment to the captaincy in 1968 Lloyd's career took another significant turn and Bond made no shrewder nor more effective move than the promotion of Lloyd and Barry Wood as his opening partnership, though it was some time before their value in the one-day game was realised and exploited.

He hit six centuries in 1972 and shared in a massive 299 opening stand with Wood against Leicestershire. He only just missed selection to tour India with Tony Lewis by a whisker; ironically Wood did go. Had David Lloyd gone East with Lewis his emergence as a Test player might have come much earlier.

In 1973 Lloyd replaced Jack Bond as Lancashire captain and though the summer was a disappointment in terms of results, the county did rise to eighth in the Championship. In the Benson & Hedges Cup match against Minor Counties North Lloyd and Hayes shared a third-wicket partnership of 227, a record which still stands. But whoever followed Jack Bond was on a sticky wicket in attempting to lift the Gillette Cup for a fourth consecutive year and so it proved as Lancashire lost to Middlesex at Lord's in the quarter-finals, their first defeat in

(LEP)

16 matches in that competition. The 1973 season also saw David Lloyd captain the Young England side against the West Indies. Clive Lloyd was playing for the tourists and his absence from the Lancashire side was an added burden for David in his first season as the county's captain.

In 1974 Lloyd was selected for England for the first of his nine Tests and scored 46 at Lord's as the home side won by an innings and 285 runs. His second Test innings at Edgbaston could hardly have been more spectacular: using his feet well against the spinners he hit a quite magnificent 214 not out.

Lloyd also had the distinction of captaining Lancashire unbeaten through the County Championship of 1974, although they finished in eighth position for the second year running. To be fair, David was away on Test duty for most of the summer and only captained the side for nine of its matches, Clive Lloyd standing in on many occasions. Lloyd was also captain when Lancashire reached their fourth Gillette Cup final in five seasons, but in a rain-interrupted match Kent had the upper hand.

During the winter of 1974/5 he toured Australia but his Test career and confidence were wrecked by the ferocious pace and steep bounce of Lillee and Thomson. Better was to come the following summer: he led Lancashire to victory in the Gillette Cup final at Lord's and was there at the finish as he and Clive Lloyd steered the red rose county to a comprehensive seven-wicket victory. The following year the side reached its sixth Gillette Cup final in seven seasons, but despite a fighting 48 from David they were beaten by Northamptonshire.

The summer of 1977 saw Lancashire slump to sixteenth in the County Championship and turn in poor performances in all the knock-out competitions. It culminated in Lloyd's decision to stand down from the captaincy after five years in charge. He continued to play for Lancashire until 1983 and with 17,877 runs at 33.41 proved himself one of the county's finest opening batsmen. An under-used spin bowler, he took 234 wickets at 29.94 runs apiece, with his best bowling return of 7 for 38 against Gloucestershire at Lydney coming in his early years. In addition to playing in 378 first-class matches for Lancashire, he also appeared in 273 limited-over games, scoring centuries in all three major competitions.

In 1978 he was awarded a testimonial and the Lancashire public responded with a figure of £40,000.

Affectionately known as 'Bumble' because of his incessant talking, he put this talent to good use with some highly entertaining performances on the public speaking circuit. He also joined the first-class umpires list, played for Cumberland and was appointed TCCB development officer for Kwik Cricket from its inception. In 1993 he became Lancashire coach, a role he combined with various coaching posts with England age-group sides, some radio commentary on *Test Match Special* and a fair scattering of after-dinner speeches. Lloyd was appointed England cricket coach in 1996 but is now back behind the microphone, working for Sky Sports.

Peter Marner

Born: 31 March 1936, Greenacres, Oldham
County debut: Lancashire v Sussex at Hove, 1952

- He scored 1,000 runs in a season for Lancashire on seven occasions with a best of 1,685 at 38.29 in 1958.
- He scored ten centuries for Lancashire with a highest of 142 not out v Leicestershire at Old Trafford in 1963.
- When he made his debut against Sussex at Hove in 1952 he was – at 16 years 150 days old – Lancashire's youngest-ever debutant.
- He scored the first century, 121 v Leicestershire, in the 1963 Gillette Cup to become the first scorer of a century in a limited-overs competition and winner of the first man-of-the-match award.

LANCASHIRE RECORD	
BATTING	
M	236
I	391
NO	38
Runs	10,312
HSc	142*
Av	29.21
100	10
50	58
BOWLING	
Runs	4,116
Wkts	109
Av	37.76
Best	5–46
5w	1
10w	–

THE PENULTIMATE match of the 1952 season against Sussex at Hove saw the debut of Peter Marner, a ginger-haired young man from Oldham, who at 16 years 150 days old displaced Johnny Briggs as Lancashire's youngest-ever debutant. A powerful hitter, efficient slip-fielder and bowler of medium-pace, he looked destined to have an enviable career.

In 1953 Lancashire were involved in a one-day match with Somerset whom they bowled out for 55 and 79 at Bath, with Tattersall opening the attack in both innings and bowling unchanged to take 13 wickets for 69 runs. Lancashire themselves were in trouble at 46 for 5 until Marner, now 17 years old, walked to the wicket. He hit four sixes and a four in a half-hour stay which brought him 44 runs and brought Lancashire to a total 158.

Marner's best season in terms of runs scored was 1958 when he hit 1,685 at an average of 38.29. His powerful forearm enabled him to strike the ball with great ferocity and in 1960 in the match against Nottinghamshire at Southport he hit a record 44 in boundary strokes – four sixes and five fours. In 1962 he scored 1,656 runs at an average of 31.24 including 31 sixes. That season he hit five sixes and 15 fours in an unbeaten 106 against Warwickshire at Southport and a week later made four sixes and 12 fours in the return match at Coventry. He also hit five sixes and four fours in an innings of 59 against Sussex at Old Trafford.

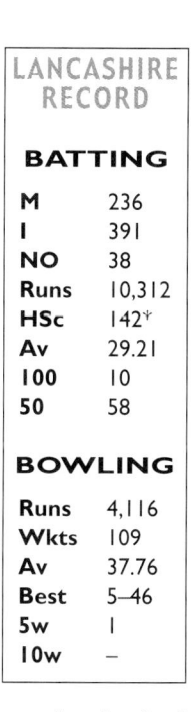

The first limited-overs competition involving all the first-class counties was initiated in 1963, sponsored by Gillette. The opening match was a preliminary round between Lancashire and Leicestershire at Old Trafford. It was scheduled to be played on 1 May but rain delayed the start and the match had to be completed the following day. Leicestershire captain Maurice Hallam won the toss and put Lancashire in. In their 65 overs Lancashire scored 304 for 9 with Peter Marner making 121, the first century in a major inter-county limited-overs competition. Marner and Lancashire skipper Ken Grieves added 136 for the fourth wicket, the competition's first century stand. Leicestershire replied with 203 all out in 53.3 overs but Marner's 3 for 49 off 11.3 overs, added to his century, made him the obvious choice to be the first winner of the competition's man-of-the-match gold medal.

At the end of the 1964 season Marner was sacked. The committee announced that his considerable influence upon the team was not, and appeared unlikely ever to be, conducive to the sort of team building they were looking for. He had scored 10,312 runs for Lancashire at an average of 29.21. This was certainly a commendable performance but there were many who thought he had not realised his full potential. He passed the 1,000-run mark on seven occasions and scored ten hundreds with 142 not out against Leicestershire in 1963 the pick of these.

He joined Leicestershire and in six seasons at Grace Road he scored a further 6,910 runs at 28.20 and took 245 wickets at 28.53 runs apiece.

Harry Pilling

Born: 23 February 1943, Ashton-under-Lyne
County debut: Lancashire v Sussex at Old Trafford, 1962

- In 1970 he hit hundreds – 119 not out and 104 not out – in each innings of the match against Warwickshire at Old Trafford.
- He scored 1,000 runs in a season on eight occasions with a best of 1,659 at 52.30 in 1976.
- He scored 25 centuries for Lancashire with a highest of 149 not out v Glamorgan at Liverpool in 1976.

LANCASHIRE RECORD

BATTING

M	323
I	525
NO	65
Runs	14,841
HSc	149*
Av	32.26
100	25
50	76

BOWLING

Runs	195
Wkts	1
Av	195.00
Best	1–42
5w	–
10w	–

HARRY PILLING joined the Old Trafford staff when he was 16. A photograph taken at the time showing coach Stan Worthington introducing him to Old Trafford portrayed the young Pilling as being unable to reach the top of his locker. He was never to rise above 5ft 2in and was the smallest man in the game.

He was nurtured after a successful school career in that tough breeding ground for cricketers, the Central Lancashire League, and played his first game for the county in 1962 after scoring 31 against Moss and Titmus at Lord's and being noticed in the Olympian columns of *Wisden* as a young player of promise. By 1966 he had won his county cap and was well established in a career that blossomed. An average of 31.06 from 963 runs in 37 innings in 1966 became 51.55 in 1972 from 1,031 runs in only 24 innings – a year in which he topped the Lancashire batting averages.

The finest bowlers probed and tested, and sometimes they won the battle but more often the reverse occurred. What was abundantly clear to all – except the selectors, apparently – was that in Harry Pilling, Lancashire had produced a batsman of authentic Test match calibre. Having survived an initial onslaught, Pilling was keen to deprive any bowler of the initiative. Lack of inches in no way restricted his front-foot play in both attack and defence and he was without doubt one of the best square-cutters of a ball on the county circuit. But two other shots brought Pilling a rich harvest of runs. On or outside his off stump when playing front-foot shots he regularly performed what can only be called an off-glide, the bat with the face turned at impact so that the ball squirrelled away through slips and gully, usually along the ground but when airborne often too fast for easy catching. His other improvised and highly productive shot was the whipped on-drive played well across line to a ball anywhere from off stump to leg and again with great precision.

For such a small man, Harry Pilling had an astonishingly good arm and could hit the wicket-keeper's gloves from the most distant boundary edge. A brilliant piece of fielding came against Hampshire at Old Trafford in 1970, turning a Gillette Cup match Lancashire's way from the day's first over. Wheatley, the Hampshire opening batsman who had acquired the onerous task of standing in for the injured Barry Richards, was the victim, realising too late that he had misjudged the time available for his fateful second run. Pilling picked the ball up, having run about 60 yards. His throw, which never seemed to rise above head height, thumped into the wicket-keeper's gloves inches above the sticks and young Wheatley departed a sadder and wiser man without having faced a ball! Bigger, more powerful men must have envied the strength of Harry Pilling's arm.

(LEP)

In 1975 loss of form, illness and injury had curtailed his appearances and by the start of the 1976 season Pilling was left with the powerful impression that he had two weeks to justify himself or to get out. He finished the summer with 1,659 runs to his credit at an average of 52.30 and, in a season of general disappointment for Lancashire, the slightly rueful gratitude of a club that almost dispensed with him.

Pilling batted so well in that summer of endless sunshine that he received wide support for a place in the England side. One theory popular at the time was that Pilling's lack of height would enable him to cope with the short-pitched thunderbolts being hurled by Roberts, Holding and Daniel but he was never selected.

It wasn't just Harry Pilling's height that made him unique on the cricket circuit. His out-of-season jobs gave him further claims to singularity. To ensure life's comforts were available for his wife and family, Pilling made and sold coffins, humped coal, put handles on umbrellas, fitted bedroom furniture, laid bricks, toiled in foam rubber, laboured in a gas works and was a general dogsbody in a Tasmanian cheese factory. This last occupation came during the winter months when Pilling joined his Lancashire colleagues Jack Simmons, Andrew Kennedy and David Hughes in coaching and playing jobs in Van Dieman's land.

Harry Pilling played the last of his 323 matches for Lancashire in 1980. During his county career he scored 14,841 runs at an average of 32.26. He became the first player to score 1,000 runs in John Player League matches and when he retired he had scored 3,738 runs at an average of 25.95 in 170 one-day matches.

Harry Pilling survived the fastest bowling, the affectionate patronage of the press and even the horrifying risk of being trampled to death when batting with Clive Lloyd. Few players have been held in more affection by Lancastrians.

Winston Place

Born: 7 December 1914, Rawtenstall
County debut: Lancashire v Derbyshire at Old Trafford, 1937

- He passed 1,000 runs in a season on eight occasions with a best of 2,408 at 68.80 in 1947.
- He scored 34 centuries for Lancashire with a highest of 266 not out v Oxford University at The Parks in 1947.
- In 1947 he hit three hundreds in succession – 171, 105 and 132 not out, including two centuries in the match against Nottinghamshire at Old Trafford.
- In the match against Sussex at Old Trafford in 1947 he helped Cyril Washbrook put on 350 for the first wicket.
- He carried his bat for 101 not out v Warwickshire at Edgbaston in 1950.
- He appeared in three Tests for England, scoring 107 v the West Indies at Kingston on his last appearance.

LANCASHIRE RECORD

BATTING

M	298
I	441
NO	43
Runs	14,605
HSc	266*
Av	36.69
100	34
50	67

BOWLING

Runs	42
Wkts	1
Av	42.00
Best	1-2
5w	–
10w	–

WINSTON PLACE was a steady, reliable batsman with a sound technique who played the turning ball as well as he handled the new one. Making his debut for Lancashire in 1937, he only had three seasons with the county before war broke out.

A century at Trent Bridge against a Nottinghamshire attack in which Larwood and Voce were the fearsome spearheads, proved Place's ability to take his place in first-class cricket. The West Indies toured the country in 1939 and felt the full power of Lancashire's newcomer, 164 being Place's share in a huge Lancashire total.

Then the war came and Place, an engineer by trade, turned once again to the lathe in preference to the bat. But professional engagements with Keighley, Horwich RMI and Oldham kept his eye in until he could resume his position as Lancashire's opening batsman.

He overcame the loss of six vital summers to emerge as the ideal opening partner for Cyril Washbrook. In 1939 Place was a useful run-getter, but a batsman whose lack of individual and characteristic strokes was the negation of style. All this was to change after the hostilities but in spite of a fighting innings at Oxford in 1946 Place did not hit his top form immediately. Time after time he opened full of confidence, scoring at a quick rate, run for run with the prolific, mobile Washbrook. Time after time he was out in the 20s to a careless shot or an unexpectedly good ball. A century against Sussex was the turning point. From then on he scored with increasing consistency and efficiency. Only an unlucky spell towards the end of the first season after the war prevented him reaching his 2,000 runs for the county. In fact, just that small extra measure of success might have given him a place in the team to tour Australia.

His magnificent form of 1947, when he scored 2,408 runs for Lancashire including hundreds in three consecutive innings and a top score of 266 not out against Oxford University at The Parks, earned him a berth on the MCC tour of the Caribbean in 1947/8. After failing in his first five attempts for England, he scored a superb 107 in the final innings of the series at Kingston. Surprisingly he was ignored while all manner of desperate experiments were tried against the all-conquering 1948 Australians and he was never selected again.

Winston Place (left) and Cyril Washbrook. (MEN)

Generally Winston Place was the perfect foil to Washbrook, dependable, self-effacing, capable and conscientious. The Lancashire pair became the best in the country and their combination between the wickets, with Washbrook usually the dominating partner, could hardly have been bettered. During those early seasons after the war Place actually scored faster than Washbrook. Better still, Place showed his mature sense of responsibility when Washbrook failed. He played one of the best and bravest wet-wicket innings of his career in the 1946 Roses match at Bramall Lane, putting his county into a winning position.

Place combined application with a good sense of stroke selection – a power to drive high over the bowler's head, a hefty pull and a classically perfect, smooth running cover drive. All these shots came into their own when, with 81 in 55 minutes, he pulverised the Essex bowling in 1946.

He scored 1,000 runs in each of the eight years after the war and played in 298 matches for Lancashire, scoring 34 centuries and 14,605 runs at an average of 36.69 before becoming a first-class umpire in 1957.

Dick Pollard

Born: 19 June 1912, Westhoughton, Bolton
Died: 16 December 1985
County debut: Lancashire v Nottinghamshire at Old Trafford, 1933

- He took 100 wickets in a season on six occasions with a best of 140 at 21.75 in 1938.
- He performed the hat-trick on two occasions – v Glamorgan at Preston in 1939 and v Warwickshire at Blackpool in 1947.
- His best match analysis is 14 for 216 v Middlesex at Old Trafford in 1946.
- He took eight wickets in an innings on three occasions with a best of 8 for 33 v Northamptonshire at Old Trafford in 1947.
- He appeared in four Tests for England, once taking 4 for 7 in five overs as India collapsed from 124 for 0 to 170 all out.

LANCASHIRE RECORD

BATTING

M	266
I	298
NO	52
Runs	3,273
HSc	63
Av	13.30
100	–
50	7

BOWLING

Runs	22,492
Wkts	1,015
Av	22.15
Best	8–33
5w	55
10w	10

DICK POLLARD first played for Lancashire in 1933; between then and his retirement from first-class cricket in 1950 he took 1,015 wickets at 22.15 runs apiece. Like Eddie Paynter and Cyril Washbrook, the war took quite a hefty slice from his first-class career, for instead of taking wickets for Lancashire, he was bowling out service sides. If it had not been for these missing seasons Dick Pollard could have challenged or even surpassed the magnificent records of Brian Statham and Johnny Briggs as wicket-takers for the county.

Pollard played his first match for Lancashire in 1933, having to struggle for his chance against tough competition from Frank Booth, Frank Sibbles and Eddie Phillipson. His great asset was a lively fast-medium pace combined with the ability to swing the new ball through the air and move it off the pitch. After he secured his place in the team, he was named the 'Old Chain Horse' because of his ability to bowl for long periods, which was combined with a reluctance ever to be taken off by any captain.

He took 100 wickets in a season for the first time in 1936 and repeated the achievement every summer until his retirement from first-class cricket, with the single exception of 1946, the first after the end of the war, when he was still serving with the forces and missed a number of matches.

His best season after the hostilities was 1947 when he took 137 wickets for Lancashire after touring Australia with the MCC side the previous winter. He performed the hat-trick twice – against Glamorgan at Preston in 1939 and against Warwickshire at Blackpool in 1947. Three times in his career he took eight wickets in an innings and in the Middlesex game at Old Trafford in 1946 his match analysis was 14 for 216 runs.

When playing at Old Trafford, Dick Pollard rarely joined the rest of the Lancashire players for lunch, preferring to have his sandwiches and mug of tea in the dressing-room, brought to him by the dressing-room attendant or the twelfth man. This applied even when Lancashire were batting and he was resting in the pavilion.

Test recognition came late to Pollard but here again the war was largely to blame. His first game for England was in the second Test against India at Old Trafford in 1946. In India's first innings, he and Alec Bedser shared nine of the wickets with Pollard taking 5 for 24. When India batted a second time, Bedser took 7 for 52. Pollard's contribution of 2 for 63 looks less spectacular on paper but his two victims were the openers Merchant and Mushtaq Ali who had participated in a century stand in the first innings. Pollard had Merchant caught for a duck and bowled Mushtaq for 1.

He did not play in the last Test at The Oval and though he toured Australia and New Zealand with Wally Hammond's side in the winter of 1946/7, he was not chosen for any of the Tests in Australia. He did play in the one Test in New Zealand at the end of the tour. No less an authority than Sir Donald Bradman found Dick Pollard's omission from the Australian Tests rather strange.

Though Pollard had such a good season in 1947, he was not picked for any of the Tests against South Africa that summer and had to wait until the following year when the Australians were touring England for his next call to the colours. Then, possibly to test the efficiency of the old maxim of picking horses for courses, Pollard was selected for the third Test at Old Trafford. In this game he took the wickets of Bradman, Miller and Loxton in 32 overs at a cost of 53 runs in Australia's first innings, a not insignificant performance.

In the fourth Test at Headingley Pollard took Don Bradman's wicket again in Australia's first innings and also that of Hassett. His match analysis in a game in which Australia scored 862 runs and no English bowler distinguished himself were 2 wickets for 159 runs, and although other bowlers who had been well drubbed at Headingley were picked again for England, Pollard was not.

His Test record for his two games against Australia, one against India and one against New Zealand was 15 wickets at 25.20 runs apiece in 183 overs. There was greater potential for service to his country in Dick Pollard than those figures suggest. The pity was that it was not realised, by him or the selectors.

At Lancashire he will always be remembered as one of the greatest triers who ever played for the county. Towards the end of his career he lost his zip and was playing only in order to reach his 1,000th wicket. Having done so, he dressed in his best cricket clothes and blazer and asked to see the committee to announce his retirement.

Geoff Pullar

Born: 1 August 1935, Swinton
County debut: Lancashire v Surrey at Old Trafford, 1954

LANCASHIRE RECORD	
BATTING	
M	312
I	524
NO	45
Runs	16,853
HSc	167*
Av	35.18
100	32
50	88
BOWLING	
Runs	305
Wkts	8
Av	38.12
Best	3–91
5w	–
10w	–

- He was voted Young Cricketer of the Year in 1959.
- He scored 32 centuries for Lancashire with a highest of 167 not out v the West Indies at Old Trafford in 1966.
- He scored 1,000 runs in a season on eight occasions with a best of 2,197 at 54.92 in 1959.
- He played in 28 Tests for England, scoring 1,974 runs at an average of 43.86 and reaching a highest score of 175 v South Africa at The Oval in 1960.
- He was the first Lancashire player to score a Test hundred at Old Trafford.
- He took the wicket of Frank Worrell with his sixth ball in Test cricket.

GEOFF PULLAR is a Lancastrian born and bred. He moved from Swinton in Manchester to Oldham when his parents took a public house there in 1944.

Pullar attended Werneth School, adjacent to the Werneth Cricket Club of the Central Lancashire League. Here he came under the influence of Harold Bailey who ran Oldham Schoolboys and sat on the Lancashire Schools Committee. It was Bailey who cured Pullar's early habit of backing away from the quicker bowlers by sitting a large stone behind him!

In his early days as a League player with Werneth Geoff Pullar made his strongest impression as a stroke player. Standing 6ft tall and filling out to 13 stones in weight, he hit with the unforced power of a player whose strokes flowed through a full, perfectly timed arc. Whether he was in trouble or on the attack, he employed a long and very straight forward stroke.

Pullar arrived at Old Trafford in 1954, still an apprentice watchmaker at Samuels, and was invited by Lancashire's coach Stan Worthington to play in the 2nd XI. In only his second appearance he hit a big hundred and followed it the next day with a half-century at St Helens in the match against Northamptonshire, for whom a certain Frank Tyson was playing. That same day Jack Dyson, a team-mate of Pullar's from Werneth, ran him out, a regular occurrence in ensuing years at Old Trafford.

He had done enough, however, and Pullar made his first-class debut against Surrey, ostensibly as a middle-order batsman, but he later progressed to No.3. He passed 1,000 runs for the first time in 1957, yet at times his fielding appeared casual. At one point in 1958 his county captain, Cyril Washbrook – one of the earliest and most convinced appreciators of his talent – sent him back from The Oval in the Championship match against Surrey for a spell in the second team. It was characteristic of Pullar that without argument or resentment he buckled down to the task of justifying himself. He made 199 runs in three innings (two of them not out) for Lancashire's 2nd XI and within a week he was back in the first team, a conscientious if not brilliant fieldsman. He finished that season second in the county's batting averages and thereafter his team place was never in doubt.

It was during that summer of 1958 that Geoff Pullar acquired the nickname 'Noddy'. It derived from a Lancashire game against Warwickshire: on the Sunday rest day Pullar was slumped in the hotel lounge following a rather long post-prandial bar session. Australian all-rounder Ken Grieves found him giving rapt attention to the television with the cartoon

(LEP)

programme *Noddy* showing. Yet for all his phlegmatic manner, Geoff Pullar took his cricket completely seriously. Being able to relax was an asset that enabled him to rest and refresh his nerves after the draining effort of concentration demanded by a long innings.

Pullar began the 1959 season by playing seven consecutive innings of over 50. That attracted the attention of the Test selectors who had had him on their short list for some time. Their need was for an opening batsman and he was picked for the third Test at Headingley against India. Ken Taylor and Arthur Milton had opened in the first two matches and Gilbert Parkhouse returned to partner Pullar after a nine-year absence. Pullar made 75 out of 146, the highest first-wicket partnership for England for 26 Tests.

On 23 July 1959 he became the first Lancashire cricketer to score a century in a Test at Old Trafford. His innings of 131 was a truly remarkable score and his achievement surprising considering the earlier prowess of Eddie Paynter, Archie MacLaren, Cyril Washbrook and the Tyldesley brothers.

His sudden rise to eminence earned him the position of England's opening batsman on the 1959/60 winter tour of the Caribbean. The tour showed him to be solid and sound against high pace and bumper attack. He amassed a highly creditable 385 runs at an average of 42.77 although his highest score was only 66. He even managed a wicket off the final ball of the last Test match in Trinidad after Peter May, the England captain, had given him the option of the last over of the series. The wicket he took belonged to the venerable Frank Worrell, brilliantly caught one-handed at long-off by Fred Trueman.

As England's established opening batsman, he made a career highest 175 against South Africa at The Oval in the summer of 1960, sharing an opening stand of 290 with Colin Cowdrey by 4 o'clock. But he fared badly in two subsequent series against Australia. In the interim he scored over 1,000 runs on the 1961/2 tour of India and Pakistan, including innings of 119 and 89 in India and 165 in Pakistan. The latter of the two series against Australia brought an untimely end to his Test career when he strained his groin and simultaneously tore a cartilage while throwing the ball in. He had played in 28 Tests and scored 1,974 runs at an average of 43.86.

Pullar had to miss the whole of the 1963 season but five years later, after scoring 16,853 runs for Lancashire at an average of 35.18, he followed David Green to Gloucestershire. The reasons for the likable Pullar's departure were shrouded in mystery but followed a dressing-down from Lancashire's then chairman Tommy Higson. The chairman accused Pullar of not trying and of being a bad influence. The player refuted these accusations and the club requested that he stay at Old Trafford. Cyril Washbrook called an emergency meeting the next morning and though Higson resigned a week later, the die had been cast and Pullar was on his way.

He joined an exciting West Country side including Procter, Shepherd, Green, Mortimore and Allen. With Pullar opening the batting they almost landed in the Championship in his first season. In 1970 his knee problem flared up again and after taking advice from a specialist, he retired.

Though he now retains only minimal involvement with the game, he enjoys adjudicating on the man-of-the-match award, that is when he is not working in his thriving sandwich shop.

Ken Shuttleworth

Born: 3 November 1944, St Helens
County debut: Lancashire v Yorkshire at Old Trafford, 1964

- His best bowling for Lancashire was 7 for 41 v Essex at Leyton in 1968.
- He performed the hat-trick for Leicestershire v Surrey at The Oval in 1977.
- He played in five Tests for England with a best performance of 5 for 47 v Australia at Brisbane in 1970/1.

LANCASHIRE RECORD	
BATTING	
M	177
I	179
NO	62
Runs	1,929
HSc	71
Av	16.48
100	–
50	3
BOWLING	
Runs	11,097
Wkts	484
Av	22.92
Best	7–41
5w	17
10w	1

TALL AND RANGY, Ken Shuttleworth was a right-arm fast bowler who never quite realised the rich promise of his early seasons with the county. The first sight of Shuttleworth's long run evoked memories of Brian Statham, and his magnificent side-on action with its long delivery stride was very reminiscent of Fred Trueman.

Shuttleworth started playing league cricket with Earlestown at the age of 14 and joined St Helens Recs three years later. In 1963 at the age of 19 he played in ten games for Lancashire 2nd XI. He made his debut for the first team the following summer in the Roses game at Old Trafford, taking the wicket of Geoff Boycott. However, it was a good four years before he established himself as a regular first teamer and he was not awarded his county cap until 1968, a year after he had taken 50 wickets for Lancashire.

When he wasn't plagued by an endless assortment of injuries, Ken Shuttleworth enjoyed spells of destruction. At his peak he possessed a very quick delivery with a dangerous outswing. His best figures for the county were 7 for 41 against Essex at Leyton in 1968 and his best season for Lancashire came in 1970 when he took 74 wickets at a cost of 21.60 runs each and played for England against the Rest of the World at Lord's.

He went to Australia with Ray Illingworth's Ashes-winning team and started his Test career with figures of 5 for 47 in the second innings at Brisbane. He played in five Tests for England, four of them in that 1970/1 winter tour of Australia and New Zealand and the other against Pakistan in 1971, taking 12 wickets at a cost of 35.58 runs each.

Shuttleworth also appeared in a one-day international for England taking 1 for 29, but for Lancashire he played in 105 limited-overs matches, taking 147 wickets at just 18 runs apiece. His best figures were in the John Player League when he took 5 for 13 against Nottinghamshire at Trent Bridge. In addition to his talents as a bowler, Shuttleworth also had some rewarding days as a flamboyant hard-hitting tail-end batsman with a top score for Lancashire of 71 against Gloucestershire at Cheltenham.

Unfortunately Shuttleworth's career never quite realised its full potential and Lancashire lost patience with his run of ailments. Though he was granted a joint testimonial with John Sullivan in 1975, he was allowed to end his career with Leicestershire. He had played in 177 games for Lancashire, taking 484 wickets at a cost of 22.92 runs each. At Grace Road he played in 41 matches, taking 99 wickets at 27.01 runs apiece, including a hat-trick against Surrey at The Oval in 1977, before leaving to play Minor Counties cricket with Staffordshire.

(LEP)

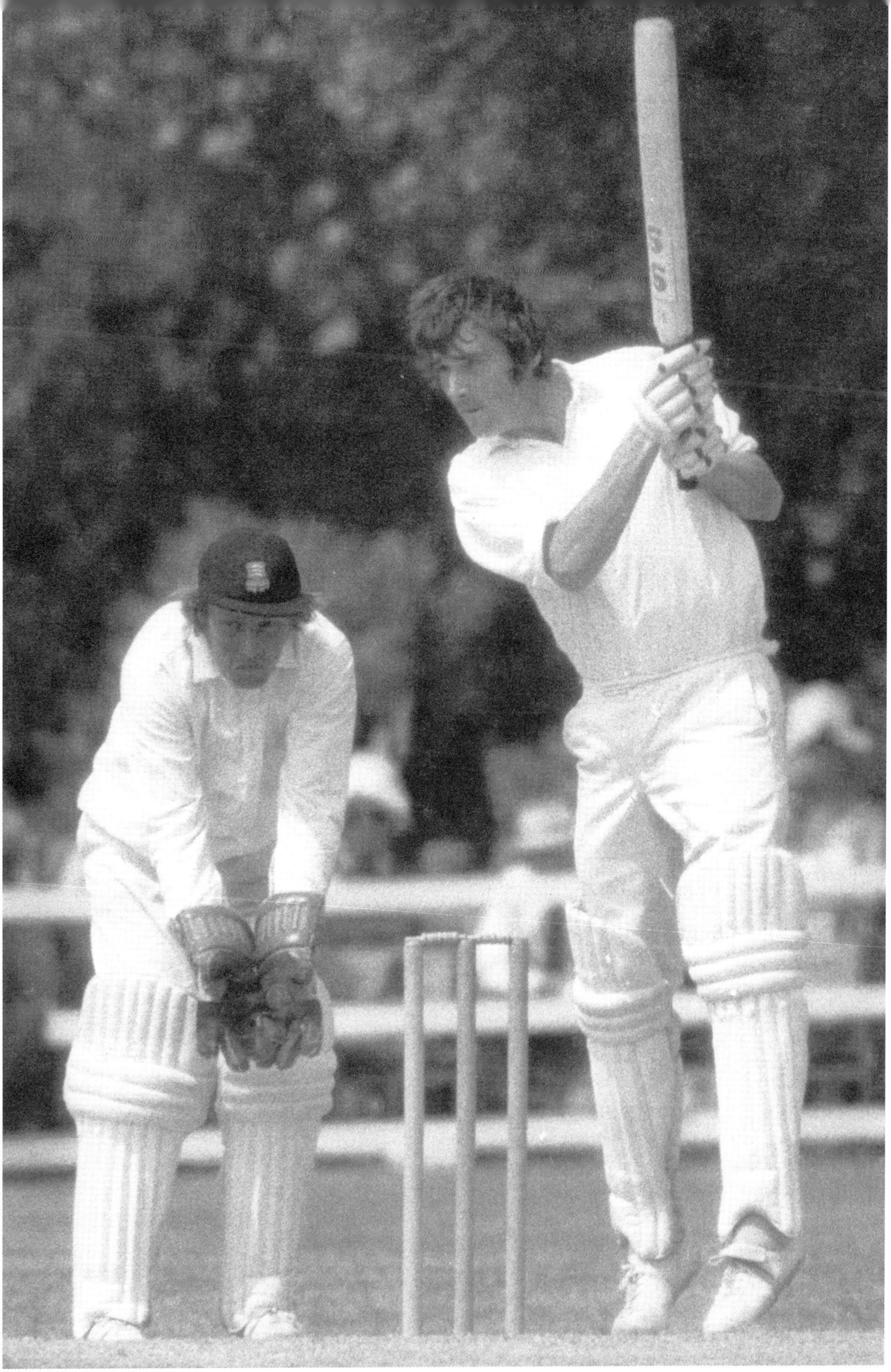

(LEP)

Jack Simmons

Born: 28 March 1941, Clayton-le-Moors
County debut: Lancashire v Northamptonshire at Blackpool, 1968

LANCASHIRE RECORD	
BATTING	
M	429
I	530
NO	142
Runs	8,773
HSc	112
Av	22.61
100	5
50	38
BOWLING	
Runs	26,489
Wkts	985
Av	26.89
Best	7–64
5w	40
10w	6

- His best bowling for Lancashire is 7 for 64 v Hampshire at Southport in 1973.
- He scored five centuries for Lancashire with a highest of 112 v Sussex at Hove in 1970.
- He performed the hat-trick v Nottinghamshire at Liverpool in 1977, finishing with 5 for 8.
- He led Tasmania to Gillette Cup glory in 1979 and his best bowling for them was 7 for 59 v Queensland at Brisbane in 1978/9.
- He was appointed chairman of Lancashire's cricket committee in 1997.

Born at Clayton-le-Moors of mining stock, Jack Simmons played for Enfield like his father and grandfather before him and at 12 years of age he was turning out for the Under-18 side. He plated for the club's 2nd XI at 13 and the first team in the Lancashire League the following year.

Continually in the cricket news, he gave every appearance of being a good county prospect and in 1959 he was invited to play for Lancashire 2nd XI where he averaged 23 with the bat but did little bowling, taking 4 for 36 in 12 overs. Still an amateur, he was invited to return in 1960 and it was arranged that he could have time off from work for cricket provided that he made up the hours. The arrangement was a success, even if he did have to work every Saturday morning from the end of the season until Christmas. His father died in 1961 after a long illness and with his two sisters already married, he was left to support his mother on an apprentice draughtsman's salary. It was to cricket that he turned for a means of increasing his income and he accepted a position as a professional in the Ribblesdale League which brought him an extra £5 per week. It could well have been this situation that caused him to lose contact with the county for no further approach was made for several years. In fact it was 1968 before he was asked if he would play again for Lancashire's second team.

He had continued to play soccer in the winter for Great Harwood and regularly scored around 40 goals per season, but he tended to suffer breakages fairly frequently and finally left the game: his left leg was broken three times, his right leg once and he also broke his left arm. On one occasion he was away from work with a cracked bone in his leg; it was thought to be mended but he was still attending hospital and not signed off as fit. In a Saturday needle match he scored three goals and when he saw the doctor on Monday for a final check there was a local paper on the desk with a sports page headline 'Simmons back with a hat-trick'. He was declared fit but three weeks later the bone broke again!

His county debut came against Northamptonshire at Blackpool in 1968 when he managed 3 for 44. Although he had lost touch with the bat, he had arrived in first-class cricket and began his first full season in 1969 at the age of 28. When occasion demands Lancashire's nightwatchmen bat well and in 1970 against Sussex Jack had to face five balls overnight; he was asked to see the shine off next morning and stayed until after lunch, making his highest score of 112.

It was also in 1970 that he acquired the nickname 'Flat Jack' when bowling against Yorkshire. Usually a spinner flights the ball in a county game but in league cricket it is

(LEP)

invariably pushed through at the maximum pace that will allow it to turn. Bred in league cricket, Jack used this delivery in one-day games, pushing the ball through with a flat trajectory and aiming to put it up in the block hole. Playing in a special one-day Roses game at Tewkesbury during Gloucestershire's centenary celebrations, Yorkshire needed 15 to win with three overs to go and several wickets in hand; Simmons took five wickets in two overs, Lancashire were just home and he became 'Flat Jack'.

He was awarded his county cap in 1971 at the age of 30 and like good claret continued to improve with age. He helped Lancashire to the John Player League title in 1969 and 1970, and to four Gillette Cup successes in 1970, 1971, 1972 and 1975.

He was also part of the Tasmania side who were victorious in the Gillette Cup in 1979. There cannot have been a player in county cricket who made as big an impression in another country as Jack Simmons. He led Tasmania into the Sheffield Shield and won the Gillette Cup Final for them with an all-round display the range of which Lancashire have never seen. Winning the man-of-the-match award, he hit 55 not out and took 4 for 17. The esteem in which he was held in Australia was measured by the visit of almost the entire Test team to Launceston for a testimonial match in 1979 and the state reception that was held in his honour.

The strong feature of Jack Simmons' game throughout the years was his talent to get runs or important wickets at the right time. This was particularly evident in a John Player League game against Surrey in 1976 when a six was needed for victory off the last ball and Simmons obliged from the crease with a big hit back over Robin Jackman's head.

A performance not so often recalled came at Old Trafford in a Gillette Cup semi-final tie in 1971 when he took 2 for 25 in 12 overs in a Gloucestershire total of 229 for 6. When runs became hard to find, he helped Jack Bond drag the team back from the dead with a 25 in a sparkling stand that lifted them from 163 for 6 to 203 for 7 in seven overs. At that stage Simmons was the logical choice for man-of-the-match. Then David Hughes came out and hit 24 in one over from John Mortimore to snatch the game and the medal.

At the end of the 1989 season Simmons, then aged 48, decided to retire and said farewell by helping to bring the Refuge Assurance League title to Old Trafford. Ten bowlers have taken more wickets for the county than Simmons but of those only Johnny Briggs has scored more runs.

Jack Simmons' benefit in 1990 raised £128,300, a clear indication of the affection and respect with which he is regarded. The popular all-rounder is still at Old Trafford as the county's chairman.

Brian Statham

Born: 17 June 1930, Gorton, Manchester
Died: 10 June 2000
County debut: Lancashire v Kent at Old Trafford, 1950

- He took 100 wickets in a season on nine occasions with a best of 130 at 12.8 in 1965.
- He performed the hat-trick on two occasions for Lancashire – v Sussex at Old Trafford in 1956 and v Leicestershire at Old Trafford in 1958.
- He took eight wickets in an innings on four occasions with a best of 8 for 34 v Warwickshire at Coventry in 1957, finishing with a match analysis of 15 for 89.
- On the MCC tour of South Africa in 1957/8 he performed the hat-trick in the match v Transvaal at Johannesburg.
- He appeared in 70 Tests for England, taking 252 wickets at an average of 24.84 and making a best return of 7 for 39 v South Africa at Lord's in 1955.
- He captained Lancashire from 1965 to 1967.
- He holds the Lancashire record for most wickets – 1,816 at 15.12 runs apiece.

LANCASHIRE RECORD	
BATTING	
M	430
I	501
NO	98
Runs	4,237
HSc	62
Av	10.51
100	–
50	5
BOWLING	
Runs	27,470
Wkts	1,816
Av	15.12
Best	8–34
5w	109
10w	10

BRIAN STATHAM first played for Lancashire in 1950 and in the 19 seasons and nine MCC tours between then and his retirement in 1968 he took 2,259 wickets in all matches at 16.35 runs each. For Lancashire he took 1,816 at 15.12. No bowler has taken more wickets for the county. In his 70 Test matches at home and overseas, Statham claimed 252 wickets at 24.84 runs each.

He became a cricketer almost by accident. As a boy he was not particularly interested in the game and preferred to play soccer or tennis. It was while he was serving with the RAF that he first turned his attention to cricket and it seems he became interested partly because there were few opportunities for tennis in the summer months and partly because by playing cricket he could escape the monotony of clerical duties at his unit. His sports NCO, a Corporal Lazarus, was impressed by the airman's bowling ability and wrote to the Lancashire authorities suggesting that they should give him a trial at Old Trafford. Even at that time Statham was not enthusiastic, but Old Trafford was near to his home and attending for a trial meant a precious leave pass, so he decided to take up the offer.

The day appointed for the trial arrived but so did the rain and he did not even bother to travel to the ground. Statham thought no more of the matter, but Lancashire did not forget the NCO's recommendation. Statham received an invitation from Harry Makepeace asking him to report to Old Trafford. The trial must have been satisfactory for only a fortnight after his demobilisation Statham joined the ground staff and made his county debut against Kent on his twentieth birthday. It was in the Yorkshire match at Old Trafford in August that Statham first gave notice to the cricket world that a new and exciting fast bowling prospect had arrived.

In that first taste of Roses cricket, the young player found himself bowling his opening over to the great Len Hutton. Twice in his first three balls he fell flat on the ground as he ran up to bowl on the somewhat slippery surface. He did not take Hutton's wicket but in that opening spell he did claim those of Lowson, Lester and Watson at a cost of only 13 runs. All three batsmen were dismissed without scoring and Lowson and Lester were clean bowled. To these early scalps he added those of Halliday and Coxon and finished with the highly satisfactory figures of 5 for 52 in his first meeting with the old enemy.

(MEN)

During the following winter he was sent out as one of the replacements on Freddie Brown's side in Australia and on 17 March 1951, ten months after his first trial for Lancashire, he played for England against New Zealand. Here, emerged from absolute obscurity, was a natural fast bowler.

In the 1951 season in England, his first full season in county cricket, he took 97 wickets at 15 runs apiece. He topped Lancashire's bowling averages and was to do the same for the next 15 seasons.

He proved himself beyond question as a first-choice Test bowler in 1953/4 in the West Indies where he was a magnificent match-winner on batsmen's pitches. Then in 1954/5 with Frank Tyson he formed one of the immortal fast-bowling combinations. Ruthlessly deployed by Len Hutton, the pair tore apart the Australian batting and won the rubber. Though he took 18 wickets, the abiding impression of his bowling in that series is one of constant ill-luck. Again and again – sometimes five times in an over – Neil Harvey sparred at Statham's delivery but did not get a touch. Few bowlers could have refrained from cursing their ill-luck but Brian Statham gave no hint of frustration. On figures, Frank Tyson was the bowling hero of the series; but Tyson would be the first to say, accurately, that partnership with Statham was an even one in which Statham bowled with such sustained fire that the Australian batsmen could find no rest.

Tyson could not play at Lord's in the 1955 Test series against South Africa and it was Statham who demoralised the visitors in their second innings to help England to a win that had not seemed possible. After England had been put out for 133 by the South African pace bowlers Adcock, Heine and Goddard, the visitors went to a first innings lead of 171. England fared much better in their second innings and left South Africa to make 183 to win, on the face of it a not too difficult task. In the last half-hour's play on the Saturday Statham took the important wickets of McGlew and Goddard. Monday's play was interrupted for two hours by bad light, a delay which punctuated a magnificent spell of bowling by Statham. He bowled unchanged through the innings for 29 overs to take 7 for 39 and England won the match by 71 runs.

Statham's splendid career in county and Test cricket continued through the years. He bowled consistently fast and straight and very rarely did a batsman not need to play a ball which he had delivered. There is no doubt that his unfailing accuracy helped many another bowler to wickets. Batsmen could not take liberties with Statham.

In addition to his remarkable accuracy, Statham possessed an unusually equable temperament for a fast bowler. The frustrations which are part and parcel of the bowler's lot did not upset him or affect his performance. There are those who contend that Statham would have been a better bowler for that extra 'devil' of a volatile temper. Possibly he might have taken more wickets; certainly he would have been no better bowler.

In his career he did a tremendous amount of hard work, yet he would perform his long stints of bowling with a philosophic dedication and a zest for the game that he was never to lose. Often in Test matches he was asked to bowl up-slope or into the breeze to give the bowler who might be supposed to have an extra yard of pace the benefit of the conditions. It is doubtful that any other fast bowler in the history of cricket sustained such consistent accuracy over so many years as Brian Statham.

Statham's action did not meet with the unreserved approval of the classicists but it was smooth and effortless, the run-up silent and menacing as he accelerated over the last few paces, the delivery achieved with the feet almost together, a final thrust of his double-jointed shoulder and a whip of the wrist. Statham was not a great swinger of the ball in the air but off the pitch he could move it to compare with the greatest in the annals of the game and he had a break-back that whipped in to the right-hander like lightning. Many were the wickets he took with this formidable ball and it frequently confounded the best.

Statham played his last Test match in the 1965 series against South Africa when he was recalled for one game at the age of 35. In that one Test he took 7 for 145 to prove that on the international cricket scene he was still a force to be reckoned with.

He was a magnificent out-fielder and, as one might expect of a fast bowler, he had a powerful, accurate throw and an invariably safe pair of hands. Like all fast bowlers he enjoyed his batting, summing up his own limitations as two 'strokes' – the straight-batted block and the cross-batted slog!

Statham captained the Lancashire side for three years from 1965 to 1967. He was under no illusions about the immensity of the task ahead of him when the committee invited him to take over the captaincy. To him it was a challenge and it was characteristic of the man that there was never any question of refusal. Throughout his cricketing career he had accepted any challenge that was offered and it would not have been in his nature to turn his back on this one. He had intended to continue to play until the end of June 1968 but he postponed his final appearance for Lancashire so that he could take part in the Roses match at Old Trafford in August. Statham took the Yorkshire batting by the scruff of the neck to take 6 for 34 as the white rose county were bowled out for 61.

After his retirement from first-class cricket, Statham received offers from league clubs but refused them all, taking the view that he would not be happy bowling flat out against youngsters starting out on their cricketing career.

Made a CBE in 1966 for his services to cricket, Brian Statham was one of the all-time greats.

Roy Tattersall

Born: 17 August 1922, Bolton
County debut: Lancashire v Glamorgan at Old Trafford, 1948

LANCASHIRE RECORD	
BATTING	
M	277
I	312
NO	128
Runs	1,786
HSc	58
Av	9.70
100	–
50	1
BOWLING	
Runs	20,316
Wkts	1,168
Av	17.39
Best	9–40
5w	83
10w	16

- He took 100 wickets in a season on seven occasions with a best of 171 at 13.29 in 1950 when he headed the national averages.
- He performed the hat-trick v Nottinghamshire at Old Trafford in 1953 and went on to take 7 wickets for 0 runs in the course of 19 balls. His final analysis was 9 for 40 and he had match figures of 14 for 73.
- He appeared for England in 16 Tests with a best return of 7 for 52 v South Africa at Lord's in 1951.

AFTER PLAYING with Tonge and Bradshaw in the Bolton League, Roy Tattersall joined Lancashire for a career that effectively spanned only nine seasons during which he took 1,168 wickets for the county. His bowling average of 17.39 is lower than that of Jim Laker, lower indeed than any post-war off-spinner who took more than 1,000 wickets and between the wars only George Macauley of Yorkshire took his wickets more cheaply.

Between 1951 and 1954 Tattersall played 16 times for England, taking 58 wickets at 26.18 runs apiece; many better known bowlers have produced much less.

He joined Lancashire in 1948 at the comparatively advanced age of 25. With Pollard and Phillipson reaching the end of their time, Lancashire's main priority was to find new-ball bowlers and the tall Tattersall's ability to swing the ball away at medium-pace gave him possibilities in this area. His career started quietly enough: he bowled 149 overs in 1948 taking 14 wickets and in the following year was given rather more opportunity, bowling over 400 overs and taking 36 wickets. Then before the start of the 1950 season, the Lancashire Committee made a decision which thrust him through the rank and file of county bowlers.

Forsaking seam-up for spin, Tattersall started 1950 quietly, but his 6 for 69 at Edgbaston on 20 May had much to do with Lancashire's victory. In the next match at Sheffield his 5 for 60 in Yorkshire's second innings, which included the wickets of Hutton, Halliday and Ted Lester, enabled Lancashire to squeeze home by 14 runs. From then on the season became a personal triumph. He took 171 wickets in the Championship alone and his total haul of 193 wickets at 13.59 runs apiece put him comfortably at the top of the national bowling averages.

Tatt's Test debut came when, together with the youthful Statham, he flew out to Australia to reinforce Freddie Brown's beleaguered troops in 1950/1. He had little opportunity to become acclimatised to Australian conditions before he was thrust into the crucible at Adelaide in the fourth Test. Under these circumstances he did not succeed in reproducing his form of the summer. He claimed the wickets of Morris (a double centurion), Burke and Tallon in Australia's first innings for 95 runs. Perhaps bowling at the Australians taught him technique for it was with his batting in the last Test at Melbourne that he made some impact on the series. Tattersall was under no illusions about his style. He would clamp his back foot firmly inside the crease and dart forward with his bat towards the pitch of the ball, frequently more in fervent hope than from mature judgment. However, the 'method' worked well enough at Melbourne, as it had worked in similar tight situations at Old Trafford and on other English cricket fields. When Tattersall came to the wicket England were 246 for 9, only 29 runs ahead of the Australian first innings total. Nothing much was expected of Tattersall as he walked out to join Reg Simpson who had been in since the fall of the first wicket. Against all expectations, however, Tattersall stayed with Simpson while 74 almost incredible runs were added for the last wicket, runs that completely changed the course of the game. England's ultimate lead of 103 runs was enough to give them their first win over Australia since The Oval Test of 1938. When England moved on, his 6 for 44 in New Zealand's second innings in the second Test gave the team an easy victory.

In 1951 he played in all five Tests against South Africa, taking 21 at 20.90. A rain-damaged wicket at Lord's gave him an opportunity which he did not spurn: he took 7 for 52 and with 5 for 49 in the second he bowled England to victory by ten wickets. He was a key member of the England party that toured India in 1951/2. In the drawn series he bowled nearly twice as many overs as anyone else, taking 21 wickets at 28.33 on unresponsive pitches. Strangely, this excellent performance effectively marked the end of his Test career.

In 1952 Tattersall took 145 wickets at 17.70 runs each but was not selected for any of the Tests. In the following season he took 164 wickets, recording the remarkable match analysis of 14 for 73 including a hat-trick in the match against Nottinghamshire at Old Trafford, but he only played in one Test. Another good season in 1954, when he took 117 wickets at less than 17 runs apiece, earned him one Test against Pakistan. This was to be his last appearance for England but he continued to be an integral part of Lancashire's attack. In 1955, a batsman's summer, his 124 wickets cost nearly 22 runs each but more favourable conditions in 1956 saw him bowling brilliantly again. In the Whitsun match against Yorkshire at Headingley he took 14 for 90, bowling Lancashire to victory by 153 runs. By mid-July Lancashire were hot on Surrey's heels; Tattersall had taken 91 wickets, lay third in the national bowling averages and had a chance of being the first to 100 wickets. At this point Lancashire, in their wisdom, decided to omit their most successful bowler from seven Championship games!

The county failed to force victory in four of these games. Tatt was recalled and in Lancashire's last five matches he took 26 wickets. In the crucial match against Surrey at The Oval in late August he took 6 for 32, Surrey being bowled out for 96, but with Lancashire in a strong position, rain washed out the last two days. Later he was selected to play for The Rest against Surrey, by then county champions, and his figures of 2 for 17 and 6 for 29 further emphasised Lancashire's folly in dropping him.

In 1957 he took 135 wickets at 18.02 and in 1958 had 94 at 17.90. However, he was left out of the side for five Championship matches in 1958 and his career at Old Trafford seemed to be nearing its end. So it proved, for in 1959 Tattersall made only one Championship appearance and that in late August. Though he played a few games in 1960 he was not re-engaged at the end of the season. This was a sad and unaccountable end to a most distinguished career.

Cyril Washbrook

Born: 6 December 1914, Barrow near Clitheroe
Died: 27 April 1999
County debut: Lancashire v Sussex at Old Trafford, 1933

- He passed 1,000 runs in a season on 15 occasions with a best of 1,938 at 71.77 in 1946, including 1,000 runs in July alone.
- In 1947 he scored 176 and 121 not out in the match against Sussex at Eastbourne.
- He carried his bat through an innings for 49 not out v Worcestershire at Old Trafford in 1935.
- He scored 58 centuries for Lancashire, seven of them double, with a highest score of 251 not out v Surrey at Old Trafford in 1947.
- He shared a century first-wicket stand in both innings of a match with Len Hutton (Yorkshire) for England v Australia at Adelaide in 1946/7 (137 and 100) and again at Headingley v Australia in 1948 (168 and 129).
- He appeared in 37 Tests for England and in 1948/9 he shared in a world record first-wicket stand of 359 in 310 minutes with Len Hutton. It remains England's record opening stand in all Tests.
- He captained Lancashire from 1954 to 1959.

LANCASHIRE RECORD

BATTING

M	500
I	756
NO	95
Runs	27,863
HSc	251*
Av	42.15
100	58
50	149

BOWLING

Runs	268
Wkts	4
Av	67.00
Best	1-4
5w	–
10w	–

CYRIL WASHBROOK was an adventurous opening batsman for Lancashire and England before and after the Second World War. He and Winston Place formed a formidable opening pair for the red rose county while Washbrook's Test career is remembered principally for his partnerships with Yorkshire's Len Hutton.

At school, both at Barrow near Clitheroe and at Bridgnorth in Shropshire, Washbrook was considered something of a cricketing prodigy. He spent much of his spare time during the summer at the nets of the local clubs and at Bridgnorth Grammar School. It was not long before he was playing for the school 1st XI and also for the 2nd XI of the local club. From the club second team he soon progressed to the 1st XI and in his first summer at Bridgnorth he scored well over 1,000 runs playing for both teams. Scouts from Lancashire, Warwickshire and Worcestershire offered him games with their minor county sides and ultimately at the age of 16 he was offered terms to join the respective ground staffs.

His father wanted him to stay on at school with a view to university entrance. However, he failed to get into Birmingham University, where he would have taken a degree in brewing, only because he had not done a written paper in art. If he had gone to university, he would have joined Warwickshire as an amateur. Instead he went straight from school to join Lancashire as a professional.

He used to enjoy telling the story of his arrival at Old Trafford station in April 1933, only his second visit to the ground. A tall man carrying a bag had also left the train and the 18-year-old Washbrook asked if he could direct him to the ground's main entrance. The man said he was going there and would show him the way. 'What are you, a batsman or a bowler?' he asked the club's latest recruit. 'A batsman,' said Washbrook. 'There's not much chance for batsmen here,' grunted the man who turned out to be the great Sydney Barnes, then aged 60 and a bowling coach at Old Trafford.

Washbrook came under the shrewd eye of Harry Makepeace and recorded in his autobiography the debt he owed Makepeace for the old cricketer's wise counsel and the care he took to ensure that the youngster had adequate practice at the nets against all types of bowling.

(LEP)

His first game as a member of the ground staff was a testing match with Yorkshire 2nd XI at Bradford in the summer of 1933. He distinguished himself by scoring an unbeaten 202. Playing in the same game was a young Yorkshireman some 18 months younger named Leonard Hutton. More than a decade and a world war later the two men were to open the England innings together.

Washbrook's first appearance for the county side was against Sussex at Old Trafford. He batted at No.5 in the first innings and was out leg-before for 7. In the second, with a draw inevitable, he was sent in first and scored 40, hooking and cutting the renowned Maurice Tate with an assurance almost amounting to impudence. His next first-class game was against Surrey, also at Old Trafford. Alf Gover was the fastest bowler he had faced at that time, redoubtable, persevering and accurate. In a remarkable innings, not conspicuously noted for its orthodoxy, the young Washbrook scored 152 and went to his first county century with four successive boundaries. But this was not to be a story of continuous success. In his next three games, batting lower down the order, his aggregate was only 15. He returned to form, however, against the West Indian tourists at Aigburth, scoring 95 himself and taking part with Len Hopwood in a stand of 200.

For Washbrook the 1935 season was the summer of decision. He had to succeed in keeping his place in the county side or, in accordance with the arrangements he had made with his father, turn his attentions to another means of earning a living. Happily for him – and for Lancashire and English cricket – his natural grit and talent overcame all hazards. In a game at The Parks against Oxford University he scored 228 out of 431. Against Worcestershire, facing Perks at his quickest and batting first on a lively wicket, he carried his bat through both Lancashire innings and was awarded his county cap.

Lancashire did not have a particularly good season in 1936 and though Washbrook scored more than 1,000 runs, including centuries against the Indian tourists and Somerset, he could hardly be said to have fulfilled the promise of previous years. He did not start any more profitably in 1937 and after a string of indifferent scores, he was put back into the second team to give him an opportunity to regain his confidence. At last he scored a hundred in a Minor Counties game and back he went into the county side. In his first game on his return he scored 72 against Leicestershire and followed that up with an unbeaten 121 at Northampton. His next ten innings included a hundred against Surrey at Old Trafford and two against Sussex at Aigburth and Hove. In six matches he scored 670 runs and his run of success gained him a late place in The Oval test match against New Zealand when Eddie Paynter was obliged to withdraw through injury.

In the two seasons immediately preceding the war, Washbrook consolidated his place in the Lancashire team. He hit five centuries in 1938 including an unbeaten double century against Gloucestershire at Bristol but he was not invited to play in a representative game and in the Test series with Australia it was his Lancashire colleague Paynter and his future England partner Hutton who held the stage. In 1939 he scored 1,665 runs at 38.72 but there was no century among them.

During war service with the RAF Washbrook played all the cricket he could and in 1945 he took part in the so-called 'Victory Tests' which were staged in England at the end of the hostilities. In three of the games he opened with Hutton. Twice they scored over fifty together, a significant augury of things to come.

County cricket started in earnest again in 1946 and in that season Washbrook scored 2,400 runs in all matches at an average of over 68. These runs included nine hundreds. He was picked for England in the Tests against India and at Old Trafford, on a difficult wicket, he and Hutton showed something of their true mettle in a stand of 81. *Wisden* chose him as one of its Five Cricketers of the Year.

He was selected to tour Australia and New Zealand in the winter of 1946/7. Hutton and Washbrook opened the England innings in all five Test matches, this series marking the beginning of their association as England's first-wicket pair. In the third Test at Melbourne Washbrook achieved a personal triumph, scoring 62 out of 179 in England's first innings and 112, his first Test century, in the second. Both innings were predominantly defensive, though he hit a six and eight fours in his hundred. At Adelaide the match was drawn though Washbrook and Hutton gave their finest performance as openers with two-century partnerships. Their stands realised 137 and 100 exactly. Washbrook missed his own hundred by only half a dozen runs in the first innings.

Back in England in 1947 Washbrook was soon among the runs. In that season he scored over 2,600 at an average of 68. His 11 hundreds included unbeaten double centuries against Surrey and Sussex at Old Trafford.

Over the next seasons runs flowed prolifically from Washbrook's bat and his qualities as an opener, with Hutton for his country or with Place for his county, were acknowledged and admired wherever cricket was played. With Place he participated in many a fruitful first-wicket partnership for Lancashire and the firm foundation which they gave to an innings in the years of their association was envied by most other county sides.

Washbrook played in four of the five Tests against Australia in 1948, missing the match at The Oval through injury. He averaged over 50 and scored more runs than any other England batsman except Compton. At Old Trafford he was 85 not out in England's second innings and looked set for a century when a declaration was made in an abortive attempt to win the match. At Headingley he scored 143 in the first innings and 65 in the second, and he shared with Hutton a century opening stand in each innings, a performance which established a new world record for the feat had never before been accomplished twice by the same batsmen.

Washbrook toured South Africa in 1948/9 and averaged 60 for the tour. He and Hutton set up a new record for an opening partnership in the second Test at Johannesburg. Their stand of 359 made in exhausting conditions on a hot day 6,000 ft above sea level surpassed by 36 runs the previous record set up by Hobbs and Sutcliffe in 1912. The fourth Test played on the same ground saw Washbrook fail by only three runs to make another hundred. He had hooked the previous ball for six, but in attempting to repeat the stroke, he was caught.

Washbrook's tour of Australia in 1950/1 with Freddie Brown's side was not successful for him and he was not selected again until 1956 when he was 42 years of age. He was Lancashire's captain and a Test selector and was persuaded to play in the Headingley Test against Australia. England were 17 for 3 when Washbrook joined Peter May. Between them they decided the rubber, Washbrook routing the critics with 98 vintage runs before succumbing inevitably to a forcing shot.

He played his last game for Lancashire in 1959. A master batsman, he scored 27,863 runs for the county at an average of 42.15.

After surrendering the captaincy he sought refuge on the Lancashire Committee and in 1964 he accepted the position of manager to the county side, a curious appointment which ended only when Lancashire advertised for a captain later that year. He stayed on the Lancashire Committee until 1988 when he was elected president, only the second professional player after Len Hopwood to be so honoured.

Wasim Akram

Born: 3 June 1966, Lahore, Pakistan
County debut: Lancashire v Nottinghamshire at Trent Bridge, 1988

LANCASHIRE RECORD	
BATTING	
M	91
I	140
NO	10
Runs	3,168
HSc	155
Av	24.36
100	4
50	13
BOWLING	
Runs	8,098
Wkts	374
Av	21.65
Best	8–30
5w	30
10w	7

- He scored four centuries for Lancashire with a highest of 155 v Nottinghamshire at Trent Bridge in 1998 when he hit a hundred before lunch on the first day.
- He performed the hat-trick v Surrey at Southport in 1988.
- His best return for Lancashire is 8 for 30 v Somerset at Southport in 1994.
- He captained Lancashire in 1998 leading them to success as winners of the NatWest Trophy, champions of the Sunday League and runners-up in the County Championship.
- In 1990/1 while playing for Pakistan v the West Indies at Lahore he took four wickets in five balls.
- He has appeared in 100 Tests for Pakistan, taking 409 wickets at 23.17 runs apiece.

WASIM AKRAM, the pride of Lancashire and until recently the world's best all-rounder, was born in Lahore, Pakistan, into a close Muslim family with two brothers and a sister. His love for cricket developed at school and from there he progressed into the first-class game. His first Test match for Pakistan came when he was just 17. He took ten wickets against New Zealand in his second Test – the youngest cricketer to do so. It was a taste of things to come.

His second first-class match was on the New Zealand tour of 1985. Imran Khan wrote of him: 'I have great faith in Wasim Akram. I think he will become a great all-rounder, as long as he realises how much hard work is required. His batting needs attention but he has the advantage of thinking like a lower order batsman, he doesn't have the problems of being a frustrated opening bat. As a bowler he is extremely gifted and has it in him to be the best left-armer since Alan Davidson.'

Wasim's introduction into English cricket came in 1986 when he played for Burnopfield in the north-east for three months. He was a leading all-rounder with the 1987 Pakistan touring side to England and Lancashire were quick to offer him a six-year contract. His impact was felt early on with an unbeaten hundred at the end of May 1988 against Somerset, though Lancashire's batting failed in the second innings and Somerset won an exciting match by two wickets. The match against Surrey at Southport in late July was full of incident. Wasim achieved a hat-trick and then hit 98 off 78 balls with four sixes and nine fours – two more runs would have provided him with the fastest century of the season at that date. Lancashire required 272 to win but when the final ball was bowled they were 271 for 9, so the game was officially a draw with the scores level.

In 1989 he topped the Lancashire bowling averages with 50 wickets at 19.86 runs apiece but the following season had problems with a groin injury and only played in six Championship matches. Lancashire were always concerned about Wasim's fitness problems and were keen that he should be treated like a thoroughbred and not a workhorse.

In 1991 he returned to something like his old self and after hitting 122 against Hampshire at Basingstoke for his highest-ever Lancashire score at that time, he looked to be heading for 100 wickets when a foot injury ruled him out halfway through the season. Nevertheless, he again topped the county bowling averages with 56 wickets at 22.33 runs each.

In 1992 he toured England with Pakistan and did not play for Lancashire. He topped the Pakistan bowling averages in the five-match series with 21 wickets at 22.00 runs each and a

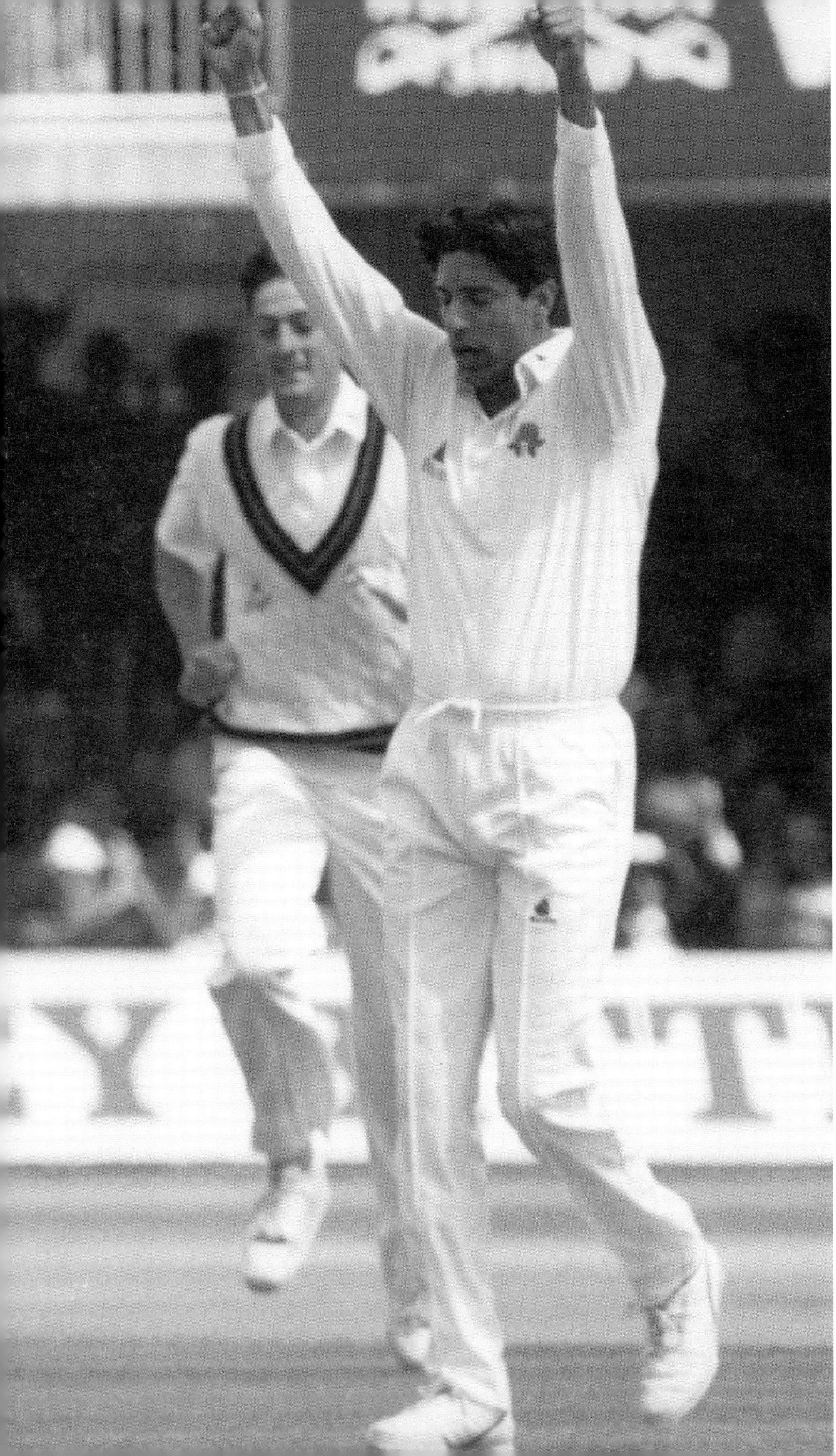

(LEP)

best of 6 for 67 at The Oval in the final Test to help his team to a 2–1 series win. At the end of the season he was chosen as one of *Wisden*'s Five Cricketers of the Year.

He returned to top the county's bowling averages in 1993 with 59 wickets at 19.27 runs apiece, yet towards the end of the summer there was talk of Lancashire seeking a new overseas player for 1994 as Akram was only available until about mid-season. But any plans were abandoned when he claimed match figures of 12 for 126 against Yorkshire, including 8 for 68 in the first innings. He only played in six games the following season but improved his figures in the match against Somerset at Southport, taking 8 for 30 and 13 for 147 in the match.

In 1995 he had his best season yet for Lancashire, taking 81 wickets at 19.72 runs apiece. He took ten wickets in a match on three occasions, more than any other bowler on the county circuit.

Now Pakistan's captain, he hit a career-best unbeaten 257 in the first Test against Zimbabwe in October 1996 and broke two world records. His brilliant innings came during a Test record eighth-wicket stand of 313 with Saqlain Mushtaq which eclipsed the 65-year-old Test record of 246 set by England's Les Ames and Gubby Allen against New Zealand at Lord's in 1931. And Wasim's 489 minutes 370-ball marathon also established a record for most sixes in a Test, beating the previous best by Wally Hammond who hit ten in his 336 against New Zealand at Auckland in the 1932/3 series.

Arguably the world's best new-ball operative when he has the golden star of Pakistan on his chest, he frequently frustrated when wearing the red rose, a sequence of injuries preventing him from playing a full summer for Lancashire. Yet when he was appointed captain of Lancashire in 1998, Wasim was in fine form, topping the county bowling averages and leading the side to success in both the NatWest Trophy and Sunday League, and to the runners-up spot in the County Championship, just 15 points adrift of Leicestershire.

In ten seasons on the payroll Wasim figured in only 91 matches for an aggregate of 374 wickets but at the time of writing the Lahore-born all-rounder has taken 409 wickets in a 100 Test match career that has seen him hardly miss a match.

Mike Watkinson

Born: 1 August 1961, Westhoughton, Bolton
County debut: Lancashire v Kent at Old Trafford, 1982

- He performed the hat-trick v Warwickshire at Edgbaston in 1992.
- In the match against Hampshire at Old Trafford in 1994 he had match figures of 11 for 87 (including a career best 8 for 30) and scored 117.
- He scored 11 centuries for Lancashire with a highest of 161 v Essex at Old Trafford in 1995.
- He appeared in four Tests for England and captained Lancashire from 1994 to 1997, leading them to success in the Benson & Hedges Cup in 1995 and 1996 and the NatWest Trophy in 1996.

LANCASHIRE RECORD

BATTING

M	295
I	442
NO	46
Runs	10,564
HSc	161
Av	26.67
100	11
50	48

BOWLING

Runs	24,002
Wkts	711
Av	33.75
Best	8–30
5w	27
10w	3

MIKE WATKINSON developed his cricket in the Westhoughton teams of the Bolton League before fulfilling his first professional appointment at British Aerospace in the Bolton Association for the 1981 season. Watkinson was just 19 years old and a relatively late developer as far as cricket was concerned. He had been no schoolboy prodigy at Rivington and Blackrod High School but his first season at Aerospace was outstanding: he scored 853 runs and took 92 wickets to win the professional's prize. After his limited opportunities with the Lancashire Federation, officials at Old Trafford began to take notice of him. His only county experiences were a number of Under-25s games and in 1982, while working as a draughtsman, he played cricket only at the weekends.

His Lancashire debut came against Kent at Old Trafford in August 1982 after Jack Bond, then Lancashire's manager, plucked him from the leagues and threw him in at the deep end. His match analysis of 13-4-45-1 included a distinguished maiden scalp, that of Bob Woolmer. On the Sunday in his debut in the shortened game he impressed with 8-1-26-2, dismissing Woolmer again and Neil Taylor.

Watkinson earned his Lancashire cap the hard way: by the end of 1987, the season he was capped, he had already made 195 first-team appearances.

His willingness to bowl whenever, on whatever and to whomever, no matter what the state of play or how tired or how sore he felt, made him a professional's professional. There is no doubt that his unselfish approach to the game means his career figures do not flatter him and are not a true reflection of his worth.

Since his debut for the county, Lancashire have had a very good one-day side. Yet Mike Watkinson has often been the difference between winning and nearly winning – a straight six to finish off the 1990 NatWest final, a blistering innings of 90 in the quarter-final win over Gloucestershire, a vital wicket to remove a threatening batsman on numerous occasions and match-winning performances with both spin and seam.

He performed the hat-trick against Warwickshire at Edgbaston in 1992 and during the 1993 season he took 51 wickets and scored 1,016 runs, the first time for 30 years that anyone had scored 1,000 runs and taken 50 wickets for the county. During the match against Hampshire at Old Trafford in 1994 he became the third Lancashire player to score a century and take ten wickets in a match. His match figures of 11 for 87 included his best-ever bowling results of 8 for 30. Watkinson's top score with the bat is 161, made against Essex at Old Trafford in 1995.

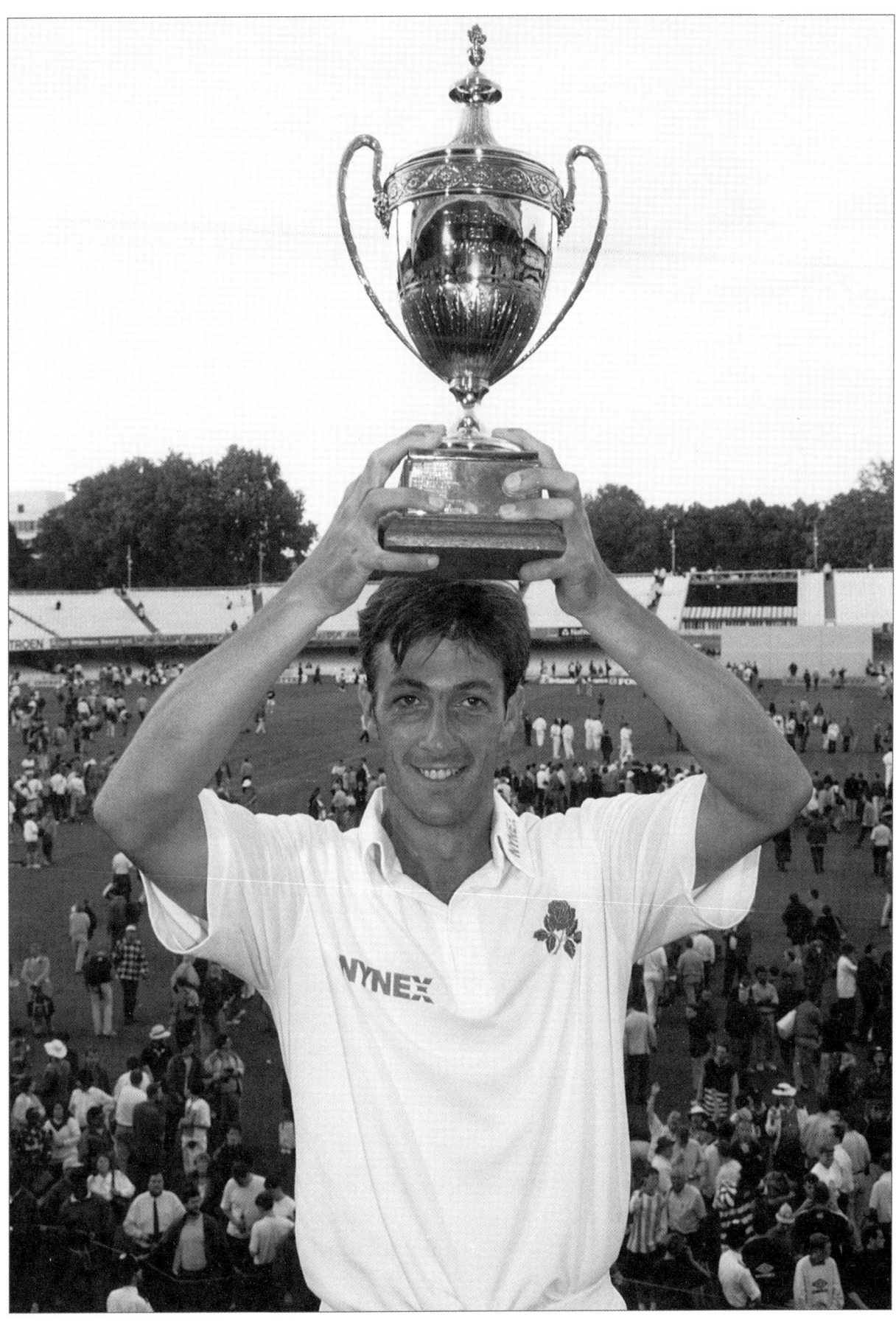

With the Benson & Hedges Cup, Lord's, 1995. (LEP)

Selected for England in 1995, his fitness and strength were testament to his dedication. If the selectors chose players for their workload capabilities, then Mike Watkinson would have been capped much earlier. He made his England debut at Old Trafford against the West Indies, scoring 37 and taking 2 for 28 and 3 for 64. At Trent Bridge he scored a memorable 82 not out to save England from defeat. If his first two Test matches were a dream, then The Oval Test was reality. Some of the press were unhappy about his batting technique, others felt his bowling featured less flight than they wanted.

Appointed Lancashire captain in 1994, he led the side to the Benson & Hedges Cup in 1995 and again in 1996 when the county also routed Essex to take the NatWest Trophy.

His nickname, 'Winker', sits uneasily on his shoulders, for Mike Watkinson, a true Lancastrian, was not quite the comic book hero epitomised by his alter ego Winker Watson of the Hotspur. After playing his last first-team game in 1999 and taking his total of runs to 10,564 and wickets to 711, Watkinson is the county's newly appointed senior coach.

Alan Wharton

Born: 30 April 1923, Heywood
Died: 26 August 1993
County debut: Lancashire v Cambridge University at Fenner's, 1946

- He scored 25 centuries for Lancashire with a highest of 199 v Sussex at Hove in 1959.
- He scored 1,000 runs in a season on nine occasions with a best of 2,157 at 40.69 in 1959.
- His best bowling for Lancashire is 7 for 33 v Sussex at Old Trafford in 1951.
- He scored 87 not out and 33 not out sharing in unbeaten first wicket stands of 166 and 66 with Jack Dyson when Lancashire beat Leicestershire by ten wickets in 1956 – the first instance in first-class cricket of a side winning without losing a wicket.

LANCASHIRE RECORD

BATTING

M	392
I	589
NO	55
Runs	17,921
HSc	199
Av	33.55
100	25
50	94

BOWLING

Runs	7,094
Wkts	225
Av	31.52
Best	7–33
5w	2
10w	–

AFTER SERVING in the Royal Navy during the Second World War, Alan Wharton was offered and accepted a position on the staff at Old Trafford.

A product of Colne Grammar School, he had trained to become a schoolmaster at St Luke's College, Exeter, but it was soon evident that Alan Wharton was a player of immense promise and he made his first-team debut for the county in 1946. He was an attacking left-handed batsman and a more than useful right-arm medium-pace bowler. Alan Wharton had a will to succeed and a determination that he should play attractive cricket. His batting was instinctive – his courage and confidence were implicit in every bold stroke he played.

In 1956 Wharton and Dyson had unbroken first-wicket stands of 166 and 66 in Lancashire's unique victory without losing a wicket in the match against Leicestershire at Old Trafford and that winter he took part in the short tour of India to mark the silver jubilee of the Bengal Cricket Association; the team was led by Bill Edrich and managed by C.G. Howard.

One of only nine Lancashire League amateurs to graduate to the international arena, his sole Test appearance came against New Zealand at Headingley in 1949. He had scored centuries against Sussex, Oxford University and Northamptonshire but batting at No. 5 after a Hutton/Compton century stand, he failed to impress, taking time over seven runs before Cowie trapped him lbw. In the second innings he was bowled by Sutcliffe for 13 as England approached a declaration. Injury forced him to miss the next Test.

Wharton's bowling was not to be underestimated. He often proved a telling new-ball partner for Brian Statham and in 1951 against Sussex at Old Trafford he took 7 for 33, aided by four slip catches by Ken Grieves who held eight in the match.

He made 137 against the 1956 Australians and in 1958 a benefit match for him saw Surrey bowl Lancashire out for 27 in the fourth innings. In spite of this, the match returned him £4,352.

Incredibly after he scored 2,157 runs at an average of 40.69 in 1959, a season which included a highest score of 199 against Sussex at Hove, Lancashire asked him to captain the second team. Wharton, dogmatic as ever, transferred to Leicestershire, proving that he was still a prolific first-class batsman. In 1961 he set a third-wicket record partnership of 316 with Willie Watson against Somerset at Taunton and scored a century in each innings against Middlesex at Grace Road.

In his days at Lancashire, he was often considered outspoken. After a particularly exhausting day fielding as twelfth man against Gloucestershire with Wally Hammond in magnificent form, Dick Pollard commanded, 'Fetch me a cup of water, Wharton,' to which the young Wharton replied, 'Get your own bloody cup'. Not surprisingly that cup of cold water resulted in Wharton coming up in front of the committee.

In a combined career with Lancashire and Leicestershire of 482 appearances he scored 21,796 runs for an average of 32.14 with 31 centuries, held 288 catches and took 237 wickets at 31.59.

He was the club professional for Kendal and played for Cumberland after retiring from county cricket. He then returned to Colne in 1965 and he held the club batting record there until 1989. He served Colne in various administrative capacities including chairman. As the Colne representative at the Lancashire League committee meeting of August 1980 he proposed to ban short-pitched bowling, a deliberate attempt to negate the impact of clubs who were able to negotiate lucrative contracts with the West Indian pace bowling talents of players like Michael Holding and Andy Roberts for the 1981 season.

The son of an alderman, Alan Wharton was chairman of Pendle Magistrates. When he retired as a Justice of the Peace in early 1993 he held the record of being the longest serving magistrate in the country.

Nothing gave him greater pleasure than when he was elected vice-president of Lancashire County Cricket Club in 1990 and rather fittingly, after promoting the idea of an old players' association at Old Trafford, Alan Wharton was elected president of Lancashire Former Players' Association in the summer of 1993. A fine all-round sportsman, he was one of only two first-class cricketers to play in the Rugby League Championship where he appeared as a centre for Salford. After a short illness he died in hospital at the age of 70.

Barry Wood

Born: 26 December 1942, Ossett, Yorkshire
County debut: Lancashire v Essex at Colchester, 1966

- He scored 23 centuries for Lancashire with a highest of 198 v Glamorgan at Liverpool in 1976.
- He scored 1,000 runs in a season on seven occasions with a best of 1,492 at 38.25 in 1971.
- He shared a Lancashire fifth-wicket record stand of 249 with Andrew Kennedy v Warwickshire at Edgbaston in 1975.
- He played in 12 Tests for England, scoring 90 on his debut v Australia at The Oval in 1972.

LANCASHIRE RECORD	
BATTING	
M	260
I	424
NO	56
Runs	12,969
HSc	198
Av	35.24
100	23
50	64
BOWLING	
Runs	6,910
Wkts	251
Av	27.52
Best	7–52
5w	8
10w	–

HAVING GAINED experience playing for Dewsbury, Hanging Heaton, Mirfield, Bingley and Barnsley, Barry Wood played five times for Yorkshire in 1964 before moving to Old Trafford two years later.

Wood came over the Pennines with the blessing of former Yorkshire captain and chairman Brian Sellars, whose professed attitude to Lancashire and its cricketers was to 'give 'em nowt'. Yet Sellars begged Old Trafford to give Wood a trial. He badly wanted to see the Ossett man wearing the white rose cap but there was no opening at the time and Sellars knew it. 'Off you go, lad. Try your luck with Lancashire but tek it easy when and if you play against Yorkshire,' were his parting words to the young and determined all-rounder.

Wood made the trip and soon proved his worth, becoming one of the most valued members of the Lancashire side. Barry Wood was Harry Makepeace reincarnated and in 1970 hit two centuries against Yorkshire!

He was a brave and combative cricketer, the sort of player any captain longs for. He was a tough, resourceful opening batsman who relished the challenge imposed by fast bowling despite his lack of inches. An excellent cutter and hooker, he was equally adept at playing defensive. His right-arm medium-pace swing bowling was extremely successful in overcast conditions and he was a superb fielder anywhere, but particularly at gully. He scored 1,007 runs in his first full season – 1967 – and repeated the feat six times in his fourteen years with the club.

Wood made the first of his 12 appearances for England at The Oval in 1972 against Australia, scoring 90 in the second innings. He toured India in the winter of 1972/3 and though he found difficulty in handling the Indian spinners on their own pitches, he took a hundred off the Central Zone. His technique tended to develop a flaw if he was jet-lagged and in the Auckland Test of 1974/5 he was bowled out first ball three days after a 63-hour flight to New Zealand from the Caribbean. He played his last test against Pakistan at Edgbaston in 1978, finishing with 454 runs at an average of 21.61.

Wood's all-round ability was invaluable in Lancashire's days as an outstanding one-day team, though early in his career, he was occasionally relegated in the batting order or even left in the dressing-room. He played in 203 limited-overs matches for the county, scoring 4,331 runs and taking 219 wickets. He also created a record by being named man-of-the-match on sixteen occasions. For England he appeared in 13 one-day internationals, scoring 314 runs at 31.40 and capturing nine wickets at 24.88 runs apiece. Barry Wood also formed a highly successful opening partnership with David Lloyd and shared in three opening stands of over 250.

He was something of a controversial figure. In 1975 he, along with Frank Hayes and Peter Lever, 'struck' for more money on the morning of a County Championship match. That Wood received a six-match suspension as opposed to two for the others suggests he was regarded as the ringleader. More controversy followed in 1979 when after receiving a cheque for £64,429 after a magnificent benefit season, he demanded more money to re-sign for 1980. Lancashire announced that he was dissatisfied with the terms offered for the coming season. Wood denied being greedy.

He had played in 260 first-class matches for Lancashire, scoring 12,969 runs at an average of 35.24, and had taken 251 wickets at 27.52 runs each. He went to Derbyshire in 1980 and a year later captained them to success at Lord's in the first final of the NatWest Trophy, the successor to the Gillette Cup. He played his last game for Derbyshire in 1983 but later reappeared in Cheshire's colours to lead their successful giant-killing performance over Northamptonshire in the 1988 NatWest Trophy.

And then there's . . .

When players were chosen for inclusion in this book of Lancashire legends it was inevitable that some very good candidates would have to be omitted. Deciding who to put in and who to leave out was difficult. The players in the following pages were the ones who only just failed to make the first cut.

John Abrahams

JOHN and his brothers came to England from Cape Town, South Africa, with their parents in the early 1960s when his father Cec, a fine cricketer himself, joined Milnrow in the Central Lancashire League. It was only a matter of a few years before the two of them were facing each other in a League game: Cec had moved to become professional at Rochdale and John was batting in the middle-order for Milnrow.

Lancashire soon got to hear of the young Abrahams, his left-handed batting, off-break bowling and tremendous fielding attracting the county's attention. In fact, in those days Abrahams used to appear quite regularly as a substitute fielder in the county's one-day matches. In a one-day game against Worcestershire at Old Trafford in 1973 the scores ended level but the visitors won by virtue of having lost fewer wickets. Abrahams took two stunning catches to dismiss England Test players Basil D'Oliveira and Norman Gifford.

Though he played his first match for the county in 1973, it was another four years before he hit his maiden first-class century, an unbeaten 101 in the Roses match at Old Trafford. It was 1982 before he was awarded his county cap. That summer was also the first in which he passed the 1,000-run mark, Abrahams scoring 1,013 at an average of 37.51.

The following season he deputised for Clive Lloyd as Lancashire captain on a number of occasions and in 1984 he was appointed on a permanent basis. In this, his first season in charge, he wrote himself into the record books as Lancashire beat Warwickshire by six wickets in the final of the Benson & Hedges Cup. Though he failed to trouble the scorers, adjudicator Peter May made him man-of-the-match 'for his overall control and glowing quality of his leadership'.

That summer Abrahams had batted really well and made the highest score of his first-class career, 201 not out against Warwickshire at Nuneaton.

He remained Lancashire's captain for the 1985 season, playing in every match in the County Championship and in all the one-day competitions, yet the committee turned to Clive Lloyd to skipper the side for the summer of 1986. John Abrahams responded magnificently, scoring 1,251 runs at an average of 40.35 but after a well-deserved testimonial in 1988 he parted company with the county he had served for 15 years. Abrahams, who had scored 9,980 runs for Lancashire, played Minor County cricket for Shropshire in 1989 and 1990, and was also a professional for Heywood in the same Central Lancashire League he had graced in his early days.

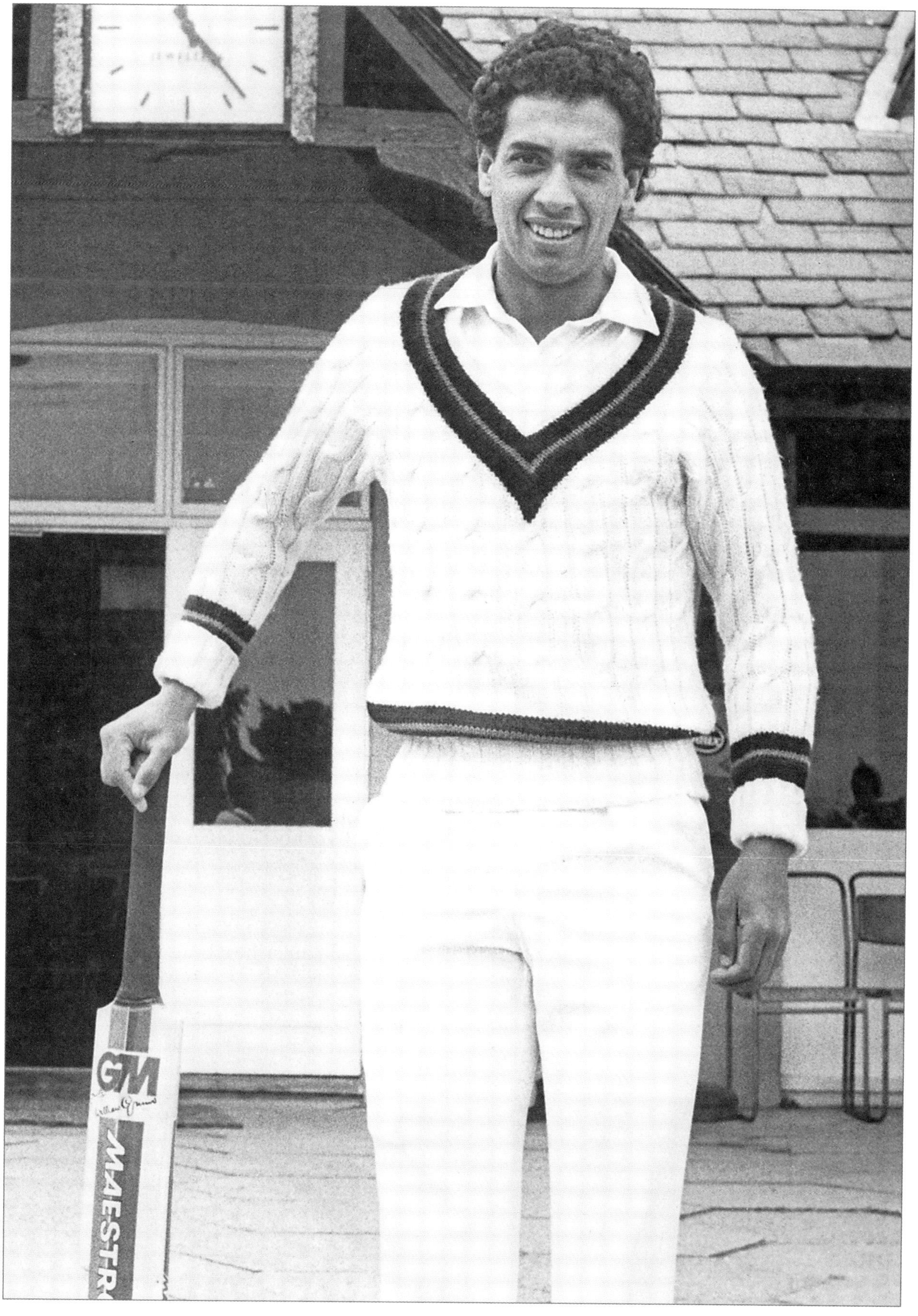

(LEP)

Ian Austin

IAN AUSTIN played his early cricket with his home-town club Haslingden before joining Lancashire and in 1985 he represented the National Cricket Association (North) in the Bermuda Youth Tournament.

He made his first appearance for the county in the 1987 Benson & Hedges Cup, scoring 80 in the match against Worcestershire at New Road. After some steady performances with both bat and ball in Championship and one-day games Austin was awarded his county cap in 1990. The following year in the Roses match at Scarborough he hit what was not only his maiden first-class century but also the season's fastest hundred in 68 minutes off 61 balls to win the Lawrence Trophy. Chasing 343 to win, Austin helped Lancashire mount a serious challenge. His innings contained six sixes and 13 fours but just when it seemed the impossible might happen, Hartley returned to dismiss Martin after he and Austin had put on 82 runs for the last wicket. Austin's highest first-class score, 115 not out, came in 1992 in the match against Derbyshire at Blackpool.

His bowling had always been economical and in 1994 he produced match figures of 10 for 60 (5 for 23 and 5 for 37) in the match against Middlesex at Old Trafford, going on to top the county bowling averages with 33 wickets at 18.87 runs apiece.

In 1997 Austin and Graham Lloyd set a new county seventh-wicket record partnership of 248 in just 31 overs in the Roses match at Headingley, Austin's share being 83. Also that summer he came close to scoring a century in the NatWest Trophy with a splendid innings of 97 against Sussex at Hove. It was this type of adventurous batting, coupled with his line and length bowling, that won him selection for England in limited-overs competition. Though he appeared in nine games for his country, he failed to do himself justice.

During the summer of 1998, the year in which Austin made his England debut, he was named as man-of-the-match in Lancashire's NatWest Trophy final win over Derbyshire after taking 3 for 14 off his 10 overs! Austin's best figures for England with both bat (15 in 1998) and ball (2 for 11 in 1999) were made against Sri Lanka and in 1999 he produced his best-ever bowling figures, taking 6 for 43 against Sri Lanka 'A' at Old Trafford.

Granted a benefit in 2000, 'Oscar' went on to score 3,778 runs and capture 262 wickets before parting company with the county.

(LEP)

(LEP)

Glen Chapple

GLEN CHAPPLE is a product of the centres of excellence which are situated all over Lancashire and are part of a Youth Cricket Scheme established by Alan Ormrod when he was coach at Old Trafford. Chapple never played cricket at school but thanks to winter coaching classes and the representative teams run by Lancashire Schools Cricket Association he didn't slip through the net.

He played his early cricket for his village side, Earby, in the Ribblesdale League. The last round of local government boundary changes resulted in a Lancashire postmark for Earby and under a previous administration he would have qualified for Yorkshire. Chapple made his first-class debut for Lancashire in 1992. An honest and genuine trier, he swings the ball both ways and does quite a bit off the pitch. He created a good impression in his first few matches with his smooth approach and high action, while his pace looked likely to increase as he gained strength and confidence. In 1993 Chapple had the chance to establish his batting skills when he scored 109 not out against Glamorgan at Old Trafford off just 27 balls in contrived circumstances when the runs were offered to expedite a declaration. It was a testimony to his character that he found his 'world' record feat acutely embarrassing.

The following summer, Chapple graduated with honours in Lancashire's Championship side, taking 55 wickets at 26.53 runs apiece and producing figures of 6 for 48 against Durham at Stockton. The reward of an England 'A' tour to India followed and he was a huge success.

The freckle-faced, flame-haired Chapple had a marvellous match in the NatWest Trophy final of 1996 as Lancashire beat Essex by 129 runs. He turned in figures of 6 for 18 as Essex were bowled out for 57, beating Joel Garner's 1979 haul of 6 for 29 as the best return in a Lord's county final. At the end of the season he went on another England 'A' team tour, this time to Australia.

After a mediocre summer in 1997 Chapple began to show signs of being capable of representing England in limited-overs cricket and at Headingley in 1998 he had Sunday League figures of 6 for 25 in the match against Yorkshire. However, he was yet to appear in the full England team.

Durham were popular opponents of Chapple's and in 2000 he produced his best-ever bowling figures against the north-east county, taking 6 for 42 at Chester-le-Street.

In 2001 Chapple proved himself to be a genuine all-rounder. In the match against Somerset at Old Trafford he produced a brilliant century and a career-best knock of 155 to rescue the red rose county on the first day of the match. He came in at 82 for 6 and after he had put on 84 with Chris Schofield, Gary Keedy joined him to produce a last-wicket partnership of 129 with the No.11 batsman scoring just 20 not out. He hit six sixes and 15 fours in his innings to equal the best-ever score by a Lancashire player batting at No.8 in the order.

(LEP)

Warren Hegg

ENGLAND wicket-keeper Warren Hegg made his Lancashire debut against Glamorgan at Lytham in 1986 and though he was obviously talented, he was also slightly inconsistent in those early days. Hegg hit the first of his seven first-class centuries the following summer against Northamptonshire, his innings of 130 helping Lancashire to a comfortable victory. In fact, three of Hegg's hundreds have been scored against Northamptonshire.

He was awarded his county cap in 1989, a season in which he equalled the Lancashire record with seven dismissals (all caught) in an innings in the match against Derbyshire at Chesterfield and equalled the world record with 11 dismissals (all caught) in the same match.

One of the best wicket-keepers in county cricket, he toured Sri Lanka with England 'A' in 1990/1 after a summer in which he had helped to dismiss 83 batsmen in all matches and represented MCC against the County Champions Worcestershire at Lord's.

He continued to impress behind the stumps and in 1996 made the highest score of his first-class career with an innings of 134 in the match against Leicestershire at Old Trafford. His ability to make valuable runs lower down the order led to him winning selection for the England 'A' tour to Australia in the winter of 1996/7. He eventually made his Test debut during the Ashes series in Australia in 1998/9, helping England to a 12-run victory in the fourth Test at Melbourne. He kept his place for the final Test at Sydney but these have been his only appearances for his country to date.

Hegg, who had a deserved benefit in 1999, has helped to dismiss 751 batsmen (672 caught and 79 stumped) in his 15 years at Old Trafford, and sits second to George Duckworth in the county's all-time list of wicket-keepers.

He was named as the county's captain for the 2002 season.

(LEP)

Peter Lee

PETER LEE joined Lancashire from Northamptonshire in 1972 and though it was obvious that he was going to be an asset to the county's bowling strength, backing up the pace of Lever and Shuttleworth, no one could have imagined the impact he was to have on the county over the next few years. With Lever and Shuttleworth on Test match duty, Lee became one of the county's front-line bowlers and in his first season at Old Trafford he helped the county win the Gillette Cup, beating Warwickshire by four wickets in the final.

No one at Old Trafford had forgotten that Lee took 6 for 17, including the hat-trick, while playing for Northamptonshire against Lancashire in a second team game and in 1973 he began to reproduce this kind of form.

The change of environment acted as an irresistible spur to success. The obvious vote of confidence that a regular place provided, followed by his sharing of the new ball with Peter Lever, brought out the very best in him. He blossomed into a bowler of very considerable class, taking 101 wickets in the County Championship at 18.82 runs apiece – figures second only to Indian Test spinner Bishen Bedi. He was the first Lancashire bowler to achieve 100 wickets since Ken Higgs some five years previously. Included in his total were two hauls of eight wickets in an innings – 8 for 53 v Sussex at Hove and 8 for 80 v Nottinghamshire at Old Trafford. In fact, in all matches Lee took 144 wickets, far ahead of his strike partner, the England Test player Peter Lever who had 87. Lee must have been very disappointed not to have been selected for England's tour of the Caribbean.

Lee was Lancashire's leading bowler for four of the next five seasons with a best return of 112 wickets at 18.45 runs each in 1975. During that summer he had a marvellous return of 7 for 8 against Warwickshire at Edgbaston (12 for 62 in the match) and produced career-best figures of 8 for 34 against Oxford University at The Parks.

In a ten-year career at Old Trafford he went on to take 496 first-class wickets at 23.82 runs apiece before leaving to play as professional with Gateshead Fell. While in the north-east he played for Durham in the 1983 Minor Counties Championship.

(LEP)

Peter Martin

THOUGH PETER MARTIN was born in Accrington, his family moved to Doncaster when he was two, so it was the Yorkshire Schools system that honed the future Lancashire and England pace bowler. After playing his early cricket alongside his father in the Doncaster Evening League, he represented Yorkshire Schools. His cricketing education continued in the Yorkshire Woollen League and then with Undercliffe in the Bradford League.

When he joined Lancashire, the big fast bowler, who stands 6ft 4in, weighed in at over 15½ stone and it was only after the excess was shed that his performances gradually improved. Once short of stamina, his fitness was such that he got used to returning for subsequent spells.

He had made his Lancashire debut against the touring Australians in 1989 but it was only in his fourth season of county cricket that he made the breakthrough, moving from the fringes of the team to centre stage.

He spent the winter of 1991/2 in Australia, playing Grade cricket in Canberra and bowling with distinction against the England team in a down-under practice match. The natural successor to Paul Allott, he began the 1992 season opening the bowling for Lancashire with Danny Morrison and started well with 35 wickets in the first half of the summer. Then his bowling performance just fell away. However, towards the end of the season he hit his maiden first-class century, 133 against Durham at Gateshead. Though he bowled well the following season, he just didn't get the wickets but he came to prominence in 1994 when he shouldered the Lancashire attack following Wasim Akram's departure for a Pakistan tour of Sri Lanka. That summer he took 54 wickets at 28.70, including 5 for 61 against Northamptonshire, and was awarded his county cap.

In May 1995 'Digger' made his England debut in a one-day international against the West Indies at The Oval. He took 4 for 44 and won the man-of-the-match award. That summer Martin also played at Headingley in the first of eight Test matches for England against the West Indies and was chosen to tour South Africa where in the third Test at Durban he produced his best figures at this level of 4 for 60, including the wickets of Kirsten, Cullinan and Kallis.

In 1996 Martin topped the Lancashire bowling averages for the first time, his 43 wickets at 25.37 including 7 for 50 against Nottinghamshire at Trent Bridge. The following summer he again headed the county's bowling averages with 52 wickets at 22.69 and career-best figures of 8 for 32 (13 for 79 in the match) against Middlesex at Uxbridge.

In the NatWest Trophy final of 1998 Lancashire beat Derbyshire by nine wickets with Peter Martin taking 4 for 19, including a second spell of 4 for 4! Sadly, since then injuries have hampered his progress but in 2002 he remains the leading wicket taker among the county's current players with 480 wickets at 27.41 runs apiece.

Best XI

Selecting a best post-war Lancashire XI is a fascinating exercise but the results are bound to be highly provocative. Different players of course reached their best in different decades and comparisons can be odious. The more I thought about all the players who have represented Lancashire since 1946, the more difficult the task of selecting my best XI became. How good a player is or has been is purely a matter of opinion, and it is certainly true that figures seldom tell the true story, but I hope the tables that appear on the following pages will go some way towards explaining why I have chosen the following players as my best XI of Lancashire's cricketers since 1946. I would like to point out that it wasn't easy to omit players of the calibre of Jack Bond, Frank Hayes, Ken Higgs and Malcolm Hilton.

1. Michael Atherton
2. Geoff Pullar
3. Cyril Washbrook (captain)
4. Clive Lloyd
5. Neil Fairbrother
6. John Crawley
7. Farokh Engineer
8. Wasim Akram
9. Dick Pollard
10. Brian Statham
11. Roy Tattersall

Statistics

TOP TENS

MOST MATCHES		MOST RUNS		MOST WICKETS		MOST CENTURIES	
Cyril Washbrook	500	Cyril Washbrook	27,863	Brian Statham	1,816	Cyril Washbrook	58
Ken Grieves	452	Ken Grieves	20,802	Roy Tattersall	1,168	Neil Fairbrother	46
David Hughes	436	Neil Fairbrother	19,197	Ken Higgs	1,033	David Lloyd	37
Brian Statham	430	Alan Wharton	17,921	Dick Pollard	1,015	Winston Place	34
Jack Simmons	429	David Lloyd	17,877	Jack Simmons	985	Geoff Pullar	32
David Lloyd	378	Geoff Pullar	16,853	Malcolm Hilton	926	John Crawley	31
Jack Bond	344	Harry Pilling	14,841	Peter Lever	716	Clive Lloyd	30
Neil Fairbrother	325	Geoff Edrich	14,730	Mike Watkinson	711	Michael Atherton	29
Harry Pilling	323	Winston Place	14,605	Tommy Greenhough	707	Graeme Fowler	29
Geoff Edrich	322	Jack Ikin	14,327	David Hughes	637	Ken Grieves	26

Left, M. Watkinson, right, S. Rhodes (Worcestershire).

BATTING AVERAGE

John Crawley	51.17
Clive Lloyd	44.94
Mike Atherton	44.41
Neil Fairbrother	43.13
Cyril Washbrook	42.15
Ken Cranston	40.16
Jack Ikin	37.70
Frank Hayes	37.45
Winston Place	36.69
Graeme Fowler	36.55

BOWLING AVERAGE

Brian Statham	15.12
Roy Tattersall	17.39
Malcolm Hilton	18.81
Wasim Akram	21.65
Tommy Greenhough	21.98
Dick Pollard	22.15
Bob Berry	22.77
Ken Higgs	22.90
Ken Shuttleworth	22.92
Ken Cranston	23.00

TEST APPEARANCES

Michael Atherton	115
Clive Lloyd	110
Wasim Akram	100
Brian Statham	70
Farokh Engineer	46
Cyril Washbrook	37
John Crawley	29
Bob Barber	28
Geoff Pullar	28
Graeme Fowler	21

HIGHEST INDIVIDUAL SCORE

Neil Fairbrother	366 v Surrey at The Oval, 1990
John Crawley	281* v Somerset at Southport, 1994
Mike Atherton	268* v Glamorgan at Blackpool, 1998
Winston Place	266* v Oxford University at The Parks, 1947
Cyril Washbrook	251* v Surrey at Old Trafford, 1947
John Crawley	250 v Nottinghamshire at Trent Bridge, 1994
Graeme Fowler	226 v Kent at Maidstone, 1984
Ken Grieves	224 v Cambridge University at Fenner's, 1957
Clive Lloyd	217* v Warwickshire at Old Trafford, 1971
Alan Wharton	199 v Sussex at Hove, 1959

BATTING AVERAGES

	M	I	NO	Runs	HSc	Av	100	50
Paul Allott	205	222	52	2,877	88	16.92	–	8
Michael Atherton	151	252	29	9,904	268*	44.41	29	40
Bob Barber	155	264	25	6,760	175	28.28	7	29
Bob Berry	93	85	34	427	27*	8.37	–	–
Jack Bond	344	522	76	11,867	157	26.60	14	53
Ken Cranston	50	57	9	1,928	155*	40.16	2	14
John Crawley	138	221	15	10,542	281*	51.17	31	51
Geoff Edrich	322	479	55	14,730	167*	34.74	24	76
Farokh Engineer	175	262	39	5,942	141	26.64	4	25
Neil Fairbrother	325	517	72	19,197	366	43.13	46	96
Graeme Fowler	234	395	27	13,453	226	36.55	29	65
Tommy Greenhough	241	298	71	1,868	76*	8.52	–	1
Ken Grieves	452	696	73	20,802	224	33.39	26	129
Frank Hayes	228	339	48	10,899	187	37.45	22	52
Ken Higgs	306	374	131	2,655	60	10.92	–	1
Malcolm Hilton	241	294	35	3,140	100*	12.12	1	5
Nigel Howard	170	234	29	5,526	145	26.95	3	33
David Hughes	436	567	107	10,126	153	22.01	8	45
Jack Ikin	288	431	51	14,327	192	37.70	23	86
Peter Lever	268	285	59	3,073	83	13.59	–	9
Clive Lloyd	219	326	42	12,764	217*	44.94	30	71
David Lloyd	378	605	70	17,877	195	33.41	37	86
Peter Marner	236	391	38	10,312	142*	29.21	10	58
Harry Pilling	323	525	65	14,841	149*	32.26	25	76
Winston Place	298	441	43	14,605	266*	36.69	34	67
Dick Pollard	266	298	52	3,273	63	13.30	–	7
Geoff Pullar	312	524	45	16,853	167*	35.18	32	88
Ken Shuttleworth	177	179	62	1,929	71	16.48	–	3
Jack Simmons	429	530	142	8,773	112	22.61	5	38
Brian Statham	430	501	98	4,237	62	10.51	–	5
Roy Tattersall	277	312	128	1,786	58	9.70	–	1
Cyril Washbrook	500	756	95	27,863	251*	42.15	58	149
Wasim Akram	91	140	10	3,168	155	24.36	4	13
Mike Watkinson	295	442	46	10,564	161	26.67	11	48
Alan Wharton	392	589	55	17,921	199	33.55	25	94
Barry Wood	260	424	56	12,969	198	35.24	23	64

BOWLING AVERAGES

	Runs	Wkts	Av	Best	5w Inns	10w Match
Paul Allott	13,434	549	24.46	8–48	24	–
Mike Atherton	2,359	61	38.67	6–78	3	–
Bob Barber	4,768	152	31.26	7–35	3	–
Bob Berry	5,900	259	22.77	10–102	13	2
Jack Bond	69	0	–	–	–	–
Ken Cranston	3,267	142	23.00	7–43	10	1
John Crawley	187	1	187.00	1–90	–	–
Geoff Edrich	199	2	99.50	1–19	–	–
Farokh Engineer	10	0	–	–	–	–
Neil Fairbrother	473	7	67.57	2–91	–	–
Graeme Fowler	312	8	39.00	2–34	–	–
Tommy Greenhough	15,540	707	21.98	7–56	32	5
Ken Grieves	6,769	235	28.80	6–60	8	–
Frank Hayes	11	0	–	–	–	–
Ken Higgs	23,661	1,033	22.90	7–19	37	5
Malcolm Hilton	17,419	926	18.81	8–19	48	8
Nigel Howard	23	0	–	–	–	–
David Hughes	18,971	637	29.78	7–24	20	2
Jack Ikin	8,005	278	28.79	6–21	10	1
Peter Lever	17,647	716	24.64	7–70	25	2
Clive Lloyd	1,809	55	32.89	4–48	–	–
David Lloyd	7,007	234	29.94	7–38	5	1
Peter Marner	4,116	109	37.76	5–46	1	–
Harry Pilling	195	1	195.00	1–42	–	–
Winston Place	42	1	42.00	1–2	–	–
Dick Pollard	22,492	1015	22.15	8–33	55	10
Geoff Pullar	305	8	38.12	3–91	–	–
Ken Shuttleworth	11,097	484	22.92	7–41	17	1
Jack Simmons	26,489	985	26.89	7–64	40	6
Brian Statham	27,470	1816	15.12	8–34	109	10
Roy Tattersall	20,316	1168	17.39	9–40	83	16
Cyril Washbrook	268	4	67.00	1–4	–	–
Wasim Akram	8,098	374	21.65	8–30	30	7
Mike Watkinson	24,002	711	33.75	8–30	27	3
Alan Wharton	7,094	225	31.52	7–33	2	–
Barry Wood	6,910	251	27.52	7–52	8	–

Acknowledgements

I would like to thank former Lancashire captain Jack Bond for kindly agreeing to write the foreword to this book, and both Don Ambrose and Peter Stafford for their continued support in projects involving the red rose county.

Picture Credits

I would like to thank the *Lancashire Evening Post* (LEP) and in particular Lisa Mault for the loan of the majority of the photographs in this book. Other photographs have been kindly loaned by the *Manchester Evening News* (MEN) or have come from the private collection of Iain Price (IP).